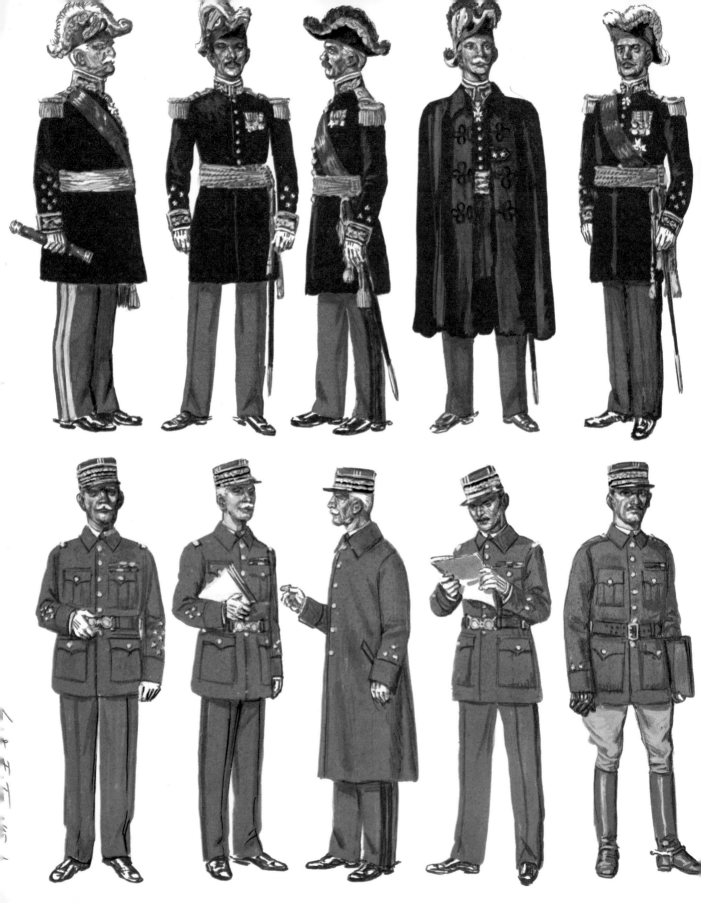

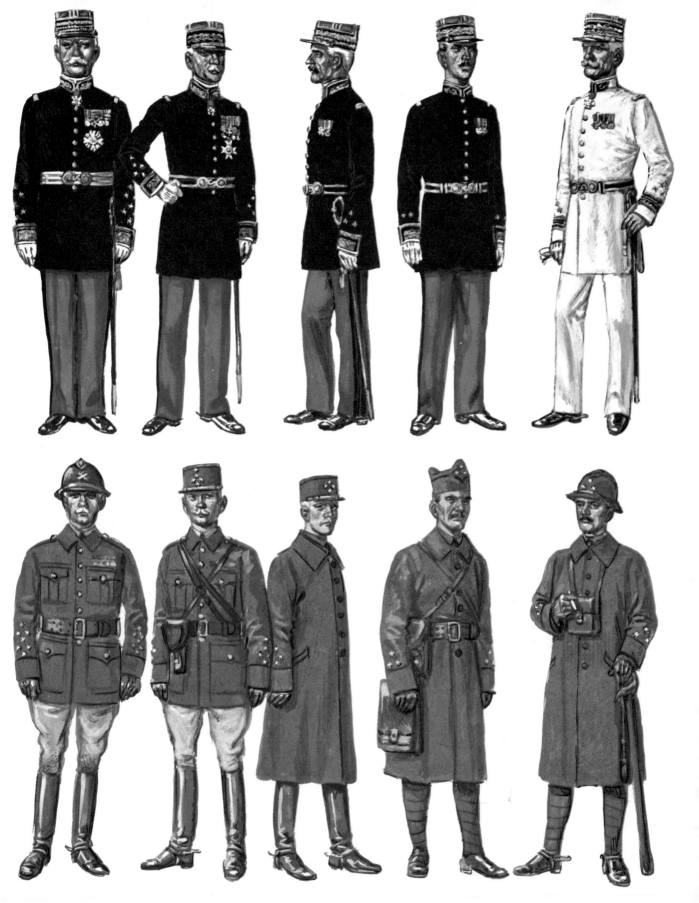

THE SECOND WORLD WAR

PART 1
France, Germany, Austria, Russia, Czechoslovakia, Poland and Belgium, 1933-41

Liliane and Fred Funcken

Prentice-Hall, Inc., Englewood Cliffs, N.J.

Contents

Foreword

In this seventh volume, the first of four devoted to the Second World War, the reader will find illustrations and details of uniforms, arms and vehicles, derived both from published works and a great number of as yet unpublished documents.

We have not included the British army in this first volume, although chronologically it belongs beside the French army. But the reader leafing through the pages will see the richness of material in the chapter on France, in which we have tried to bring to life again the almost forgotten uniforms of the men who were struck down by the *Blitzkrieg*.

Germany, with its Nazi organisation and powerful Wehrmacht, must appear as the chief antagonist right from the start of this series. The armoured vehicles of France and Germany are also included in this present volume.

It would have been tantamount to treason to have tried to accommodate the magnificent British army in too small a space, and it will take pride of place in the second volume. The second volume also brings together the air forces of the main combatants and the armoured vehicles, and shows the development of the German army from 1941 to 1943.

Volume three introduces the opponents in the wider theatre of war—China, the USA and Japan—and features the naval forces of the European nations, the Norwegian and Finnish armies and the armies of the axis satellites.

In the final volume the changing face of the armies of the great nations in the last years of war is shown, and attention is focused on the unfamiliar uniforms of the lesser European countries, ending with a review of the artillery, vehicles and machines (including submarines and aircraft carriers) developed up to 1945.

If it has not always been possible to take strict account of chronology, we hope that the reader will find enough to satisfy his curiosity about the performers in this great human drama that has now taken its place in the march of time.

The list of friends who have helped us has grown longer every year. We would like to offer special thanks to those named below, who have given us such tremendous assistance:

Monsieur Leconte, Conservateur en chef, Musée de l'Armée de Bruxelles,

Monsieur Lorette, Conservateur du Cabinet des estampes, Musée de l'Armée de Bruxelles,

Colonel Wemaer, Musée de l'Armée de Paris,

Colonel Martel, Direction centrale du matériel,

Colonel Monteil of the French Embassy,

Colonel Palmen of the Finnish Embassy,

Lieutenant-Colonel Chiroki and his colleagues of the Soviet army,

Major B.E.M. Van Boucke,

Commandant Verelst, Centre d'identification d'avions et missiles,

Commandant Servais, Service historique de l'Armée belge,

Dr E. Kroner, Austrian president of U.N.E.S.C.O.,

Captain Grimaldi, National Museum of Italian Cavalry,

and Messieurs Lion, Chayre, Simon, Dubois, Vanderpoorten, T'Sas, Moulin, Alazet, Tavart, Serlez de Leurs, de Partz, Carmigniani, Bragard, Thielemans, Guillaume, Locquet and Joris.

PART ONE
INFANTRY AND CAVALRY

The French Army from 1935 to 1940

In just two years of war the smart and colourful uniforms of the French army of 1914 had been transformed into an almost universal horizon blue.[1] But it was autumn 1935 before its uniforms had finally completed a further metamorphosis, once again in this very important area of colour.

Since 1921 khaki had been recognised as more practical, being much less visible in open country, and from this time horizon blue steadily lost ground to its less conspicuous rival. The manufacture of the horizon-blue material was discontinued, though as an economy measure existing stocks continued to be used by certain special corps, and uniforms already made up and issued continued in service until worn out.

By 1935, then, re-equipment in khaki had been completed; apart from this change in colour, however, the French soldier was still dressed like the *poilu* of 1918. Officers alone stood out from this somewhat drab uniformity, when the adoption of a special dress uniform was authorised by the regulation of 28 May 1931. The need for a uniform more appropriate to ceremonial occasions and civil receptions had begun to be felt immediately after the First World War, and several designs had been produced, with varying degrees of success, until the 1931 regulation defined the exact style.

1 Khaki had also made its appearance. See vols 1 and 2 of *Arms and Uniforms of the First World War*.

FRENCH LINE INFANTRY, 1935-1940 I

1. Standard bearer — 2. Officer in full dress — 3. Alpine infantry — 4. Colour party — 5. Drummer in prise d'armes dress — 6. Walking-out dress with horizon-blue overcoat — 7. Walking-out dress with pea-jacket

OFFICERS' DRESS

An officer wore one of the following five uniforms according to the occasion:

1 **Full-dress uniform:** of similar cut for all the corps in a troop. Each corps was distinguished by the arm of service colours it had used before 1914, which were usually displayed on the collar and patches, and on the cuff facings. The kepi, the trousers and sometimes the tunic were all in this distinctive colour. The coloured tunic became more of a problem as the tendency spread to use one standard pattern for it. An overcoat in the form of a cape completed the full dress.

2 **Walking-out dress:** the same as full dress but without the epaulettes and sabre, except by special order.

3 **Service dress:** khaki apart from the kepi. Mounted officers could wear riding breeches and boots during the day but had to return to trousers for evening dress. This uniform was used for ceremonial occasions which did not require the wearing of uniforms 1 or 2 above.

4 **Working dress** (tenue de travail): this uniform was the same as No. 3 above, and was worn in the barracks and for moving about in town when on fatigues.

5 **Battle dress** (tenue de campagne): similar to No. 4 above, it included an extra khaki shirt and tie, and a khaki kepi or a khaki-painted steel helmet. In peacetime this uniform was worn on general manoeuvres and for inspections and parades under arms.

After 1936 there was a move to make uniforms 3, 4

NB: The soutache (braid) was sewn on to the collar patches to form an angle around the insignia; from 1940 it was sewn on in an arc. This also applies to the following three illustrations.

and 5 more elegant by modifying the tunic and overcoat collars. Known as *demi-Saxe* collars, until this date they had allowed only the tie knot and part of the shirt collar to show. The more modern-looking and much smarter open-collared jacket (*vareuse demi-ouverte*) with small lapels was designed to replace this. Most regular officers soon adopted this new style but many of the reserves, whether for economy or out of sentimental attachment, stuck to the old style.

Individual variations were not completely ruled out. The new-style tunic was generally fastened with five buttons instead of seven, but many officers had only four. Sometimes the tunic skirt, for which the regulation length was 400 mm from the bottom of the belt, went to 450 or even 500 mm. The buttons, which were gilt on the town dress, had to be left unpolished on the battle dress, and to avoid the austere effect this created they were sometimes replaced by plaited leather ones. For officers who wanted to replace the rather coarse and heavy cloth of their battle dress with a less homely material there was a considerable choice of fabrics, one very much in vogue being the mottled whipcord, another the British *grain de poudre*. The general relaxation of regulations in these areas was very much appreciated and taken advantage of.

Nor did the kepi always conform to the specifications laid down in the regulations. According to these the cap should have a high crown[1] rising to 10 mm above the grade of rank on the front, and to 20 mm at the back. In many cases this gradient did not appear, and the crown itself was almost completely covered by a profusion of braiding up the band.[2]

By 1936 trousers had practically disappeared in favour of breeches in light khaki material. But even breeches did not entirely escape the influences of fashion: each unit had its individual style, some choosing to follow the British fashion, others the Saumur or Italian. Materials used were Bedford cord, twill, or other corded fabrics. Boots also were influenced by prevailing fashion trends. They were made of dark cow hide, Russian calf, or box calf, in the style of riding or Chantilly boots, as well as the traditional laced boots, British leggings or off-white puttees. The fixed spurs, or *spurs à la chevalière,* had leather straps, sometimes replaced by small chains. White skin gloves were often worn instead of the standard dark fawn ones. The regulation overcoat was generally accepted, but specialist tailors in Paris offered variations in style which were also permitted, such as the 'British warm' short overcoat with its two rows of buttons, or the sheepskin-lined Canadian raincoat.

By way of accessories Hermès designed a prestige range from which the most elegant could choose a trench stick or cane covered in pigskin or box-calf, and even a finely plaited leather chin strap for the steel helmet. This elegant range of sartorial accessories did not represent simple vanity and self-indulgence but expressed the officer's proud awareness of the prestige of his uniform and his confidence in his ability to uphold the honour of the army to which he belonged.

TROOP DRESS

Such bending of the regulations was much rarer among the lower ranks of officer and it disappeared completely when one got down to the rank of common soldier, who could scarcely manage to exchange his heavy laced boots for slightly more comfortable shoes. The arms of service varied little, apart from the collar insignia and the helmet badge.

Towards the end of 1935 a special loose-fitting 'walking-out' jacket was issued to the men; this had an open collar showing part of the khaki shirt and dark khaki tie with its sailor knot. At about the same time the greatcoat was also modified, so that it too had open revers, although the illustrated records of the 1940 period show a large number of uniforms in the old style, still with the *demi-Saxe* collar. The baggy breeches, known as golfing breeches, which were worn before 1939, were by this time however no longer in general use.

FRENCH LINE INFANTRY, 1935-1940 II

Battle dress: 1. With pack — 2. With mess tins — 3. Equipment for heavy armoured units — 4. Flag bearer — 5. Winter clothes and equipment for scouts and skirmishers — 6. Garrison dress

---

1 The upper part of the kepi, usually in red madder.
2 The lower part of the cap, the most important part, usually blue-black in colour.

GENERAL OFFICERS, FIELD OFFICERS AND JUNIOR OFFICERS

	KEPI (RED MADDER CROWN WITH BLUE-BLACK BAND FOR GENERAL OFFICERS)	TUNIC SLEEVES	HELMET, KEPI, FORAGE CAP,[1] PEA-JACKET AND KHAKI OVERCOAT SLEEVES	TUNIC OR PEA-JACKET AND CAVALRY OVERCOAT IN WORKING DRESS AND BATTLE DRESS
General Officers				
Maréchal de France	3 mm silver braid; 1 serrated band of piping; 3 gold oak leaf garlands, 10, 8 and 7 mm wide	7 solid silver stars above gold embroidered cuffs; same style for all general officers	7 solid silver stars	
Général de division, member of the Supreme Council of War	2 garlands, 15 and 12 mm; 1 braid	5 »	5 »	
Général de division commanding the armed forces	as above	4 »	4 »	
Général de division	as above, *no braid*	3 »	3 »	
Général de brigade	1 33 mm garland	2 »	2 »	
Field Officers				
Colonel	5 lines of metallic braid in button colour[2]	5 lines of metallic braid in button colour		5 small lines of braid in button colour
Lieutenant-colonel	5 lines of braid with 2nd and 4th in contrast to button colour	5 as for kepi		5 small lines of braid as for kepi
Chef de bataillon (d'escadron)	4 lines of braid in button colour	4 as for kepi		4 small lines of braid as for kepi
Junior Officers				
Capitaine	3 »	3 »		3 »
Lieutenant	2 »	2 »		3 »
Sous-lieutenant	1 »	1 »		1 »

NB: In the colonies generals could wear white full dress with the same braiding and stars as above. Officers of the services who had reached the rank of general wore the same braiding but the stars were gold.

1 The stars were reduced to 2 or 3 on the helmet or forage cap.
2 In gold: Infantry of the line, Zouaves, tirailleurs, spahis, Foreign Legion, artillery and engineers; in silver: cavalry (except spahis), tanks, automitrailleuses, light infantry, African light infantry and service corps.

FRENCH LIGHT INFANTRY, 1935-1940

1. Standard bearer — 2. Bugler in prise d'armes dress — 3. Officer in full dress — 4. Flag bearer — 5. Machine gunner in battle dress — 6. Field equipment — 7. Collar patch for blue uniform — 8. Collar patch for battle dress — 9. Steel helmet badge

OFFICERS' SPECIAL FULL DRESS	TUNIC	BUTTONS, LACE, KEPI BRAID, EPAULETTES	KEPI CROWN	KEPI BAND	KEPI INSIGNIA	COLLAR
Metropolitan troops						
Infantry	blue black	gold	red madder	blue black	gold no.	red madder
Light infantry	blue black	silver	blue black	blue black	silver no.	blue black
Tanks	blue black	silver	blue black	blue black	silver no.	light grey
North African Troops						
Zouaves	blue black	gold—*no epaulettes*	red madder	blue black	gold no.	blue black
Native tirailleurs: Algerian and Tunisian	light blue	gold	red madder	light blue	gold no.	light yellow
Moroccan	light blue	gold	red madder	light blue	gold no. and seal of Solomon	light yellow
African light infantry	blue black	silver	red madder	blue black	silver no.	blue black
Foreign Legion	blue black	gold	red madder	blue black	gold no.	blue black
Saharan companies	red madder	gold	sky blue	sky blue	gold crescent and star	red madder
Cavalry						
Cuirassiers	blue black	silver	red madder	blue black	silver no.	red madder
Dragoons	blue black	silver	red madder	blue black	silver no.	white
Mounted dragoons	blue black	silver	red madder	blue black	silver no. and star	white
Light cavalry	blue black	silver	red madder	sky blue	silver no.	sky blue
Hussars	blue black	silver	red madder	sky blue	silver no.	sky blue
Automitrailleuses	blue black	silver	red madder	sky blue	silver no.	sky blue
North African cavalry						
African light cavalry	sky blue	silver	red madder	sky blue	silver no.	light yellow
Remounts	red madder	gold	red madder	sky blue	gold no.	red madder
Cavalry school	blue black	silver	red madder	sky blue	silver, no. in centre of voided grenade	sky blue
Algerian and Tunisian spahis	red madder	gold	red madder	sky blue	gold no.	red madder
Moroccan spahis	red madder	gold	red madder	sky blue	gold no. and seal of Solomon	red madder
Foreign regiment	blue black	silver	red madder	blue black	no. in silver grenade	blue black

FRENCH ALPINE LIGHT INFANTRY, 1935-1940

1. Mounted officer (only officers wore the beret at an angle over the right ear) — 2. Summer manoeuvres dress — 3. Standard bearer — 4. Prise d'armes dress — 5. Bugler — 6. Mountain dress with steel helmet

	TUNIC	BUTTONS, LACE, KEPI BRAID EPAULETTES	KEPI CROWN	KEPI BAND	KEPI INSIGNIA	COLLAR
Artillery	blue black	gold	blue black	blue black	gold no.	scarlet
Engineers	blue black	gold	blue black	blue black	gold no.	blue black
Baggage train	blue black	silver	red madder	blue black	silver no.	scarlet
Gendarmerie	blue black	silver	blue black	blue black	silver grenade	blue black
Garde républicaine mobile	blue black	gold	blue black	blue black	gold grenade	blue black
Garde républicaine de Paris	blue black	gold	blue black	blue black	gold grenade	blue black
Sapeurs-pompiers de la ville de Paris	blue black	gold	dark blue	black velvet	golde grenade	blue black
Services						
Medical corps	blue black	gold	red madder	crimson velvet	gold badge	crimson velvet
Pharmacists	blue black	gold	red madder	green velvet	gold badge	green velvet
Dentists	blue black	gold	red madder	brown velvet	gold badge	plum velvet
Veterinary surgeons	blue black	silver	red madder	garnet velvet	silver badge	garnet velvet
Commissariat	blue black	silver	red madder	blue black	silver badge	blue black
Administration	blue black	gold	red madder	blue black	gold badge	blue black
Military justice	blue black	gold	blue black	blue black	gold badge	black velvet
Overseas troops						
Infantry	blue black	gold	red madder	blue black	gold anchor	blue black
Artillery	blue black	gold	red madder	blue black	gold badge	scarlet
Services						
Medical corps	blue black	gold	blue black	crimson velvet	gold badge	crimson velvet
Pharmacists	blue black	gold	blue black	green velvet	gold badge	green velvet
Commissariat	blue black	silver	red madder	blue black	silver anchor	blue black
Administration	blue black	gold	blue black	blue black	gold anchor	blue black

FRENCH ARMY, RANKS (Official Bulletin 1937)

Kepis and cuffs in peacetime: 1. Colonel — 2. Lieutenant-colonel — 3. Commandant — 4. Capitaine — 5. Lieutenant — 6. Sous-lieutenant — 7. Adjudant-chef — 8. Adjudant — 9. Sergent-chef and maréchal des logis-chef — 10. Sergent and maréchal des logis admitted to the corps of regular sous-officiers — 11. Sergent and maréchal des logis — 12. Caporal-chef and brigadier-chef — 13. Caporal and brigadier — 14. Soldat de 1re classe

NB: In the mounted sections and in the artillery the ranks of maréchal des logis and brigadier corresponded to those of sergent and caporal. The arm of service colour, seen in 11, 12, 13 and 14 at the bottom of the sleeves and under the stripes was red for the infantry, green for tanks, dark blue for cavalry, and red or scarlet for the other arms.

15 to 28. Rank insignia on battle dress, in the same order as above. The stripes varied according to the colour of the buttons, thus for cavalry they were silver.

29. Kepi of chef de bataillon, line infantry — 30. Kepi of sous-lieutenant, tanks — 31–32. Infantry capitaine in full dress, front and back — 33. Commandant, battle dress — 34. Capitaine in battle dress

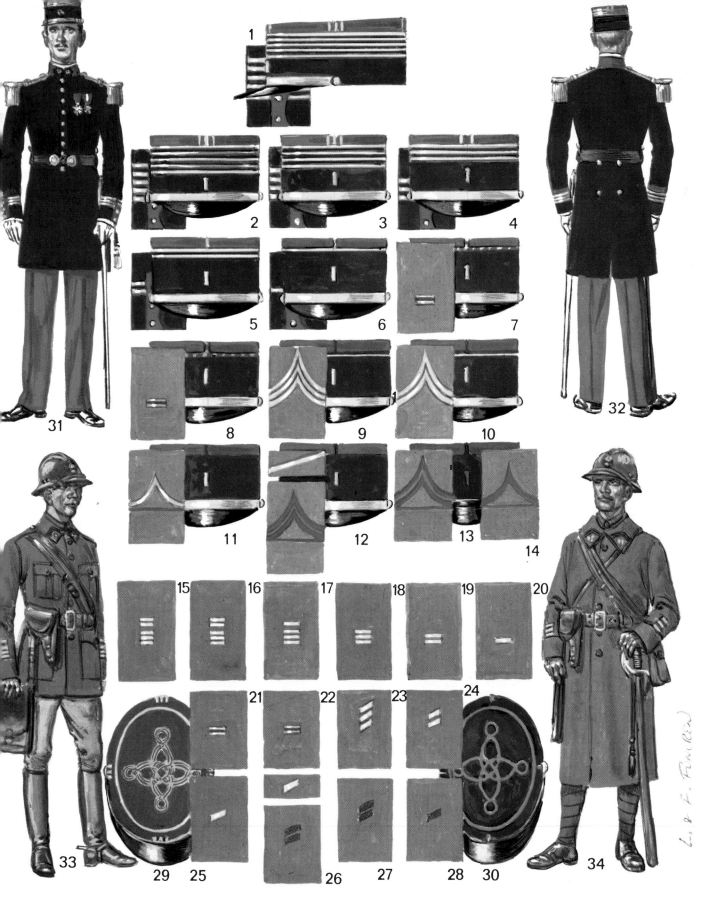

1

2

3

4

5

6

7

8

9

10

11

12

13

14

15 16 17 18 19 20

21 22 23 24

29 25

26 27 28 30

31

32

33

34

	COLLAR PATCHES	COLLAR INSIGNIA	CUFF FACINGS	TROUSERS	TROUSER STRIPES OR PIPING	BELT BUCKLE
Metropolitan troops						
Infantry	blue black	gold no.	red madder	red madder	blue-black stripe	gold
Light infantry	blue black	silver horn and no.	blue black	dark iron grey	light-yellow piping	silver
Tanks	blue black	silver no.	light grey	dark blue	light-grey stripe	silver
North African Troops						
Zouaves	blue black	gold no.	none	red madder	blue-black stripe	gold
Native tirailleurs: Algerian and Tunisian	light blue	gold no.	none	red madder	light-blue stripe	gold
Moroccan	light blue	gold no. and seal of Solomon	light yellow	red madder	light-blue stripe	gold
African light infantry	blue black with light-yellow piping	silver no.	blue black	red madder	blue-black stripe	silver
Foreign Legion	blue black with green braid	gold no. in grenade	blue black	red madder	blue-black stripe	gold
Saharan companies	red madder	gold star and crescent	red madder	sky blue	double stripe of red madder	gold
Cavalry						
Cuirassiers	blue black	silver no.	red madder	red madder	blue-black stripe	silver
Dragoons	blue black	silver no.	white	red madder	blue-black stripe	silver
Mounted dragoons	blue black	silver no. and star	white	red madder	blue-black stripe	silver
Light cavalry	sky blue with silver piping	silver no.	sky blue	red madder	double stripe of sky blue	silver
Hussars	sky blue, no piping	silver no.	sky blue	red madder	double stripe of sky blue	silver
Automitrailleuses	sky blue with purple piping	silver no.	sky blue	red madder	double stripe of sky blue	silver

FRENCH MILITARY ACADEMIES

Saint-Cyr: 1. Officer, full dress — 2. Caporal, full dress — 3. Officer's shako (infantry) — 4. Officer's shako (cavalry) — 5. Shako badge (usually hidden by the plume) — 6. Steel helmet insignia. As on 5, the ribbon bears the inscription *École spéciale militaire* — 7. Indoor dress — 8. Collar patch, a yellow grenade on a blue or khaki ground according to rank — 9–10. Undress collar and kepi — 11. Cadet, Marching column of cadet reserve officers

12–13. École polytechnique: hat (right side) and cadet — 14–15. École militaire de Saumur for cavalry and baggage train: Sous-officier for riding and officer-instructor in horsemanship in full riding dress — 16. Cadet from the École de Saint-Maixent — 17. Cadet from the École du Service de santé militaire (military school of medicine) — 18. Kepi, collar, cuff facings and insignia of a cadet pharmacist

1

3

4

2

7

8

5

6

9

10

12

11

14

15

16

17

13

18

F. FUNCKEN

	COLLAR PATCHES	COLLAR INSIGNIA	CUFF FACINGS	TROUSERS	TROUSER STRIPES OR PIPING	BELT BUCKLE
North African cavalry						
African light cavalry	sky blue	silver no.	light yellow	red madder	double stripe of sky blue	silver
Remounts	blue black	gold no.	red madder	sky blue	double stripe of red madder	gold
Cavalry school	blue black	silver, no. in centre of voided grenade	sky blue	red madder	double stripe of sky blue	silver
Algerian and Tunisian spahis	red madder	gold no.	red madder	sky blue	double stripe of red madder	gold
Moroccan spahis	red madder	gold no. and seal of Solomon	red madder	sky blue	double stripe of red madder	gold
Foreign regiment	blue black with green piping	silver no. in grenade	blue black	red madder	black stripe	silver
Artillery	blue black	gold no.	scarlet	blue black	double stripe of scarlet	gold
Engineers	blue black with scarlet piping	gold no.	blue black	blue black	double stripe of scarlet	gold
Baggage train	dark green	silver no.	scarlet	red madder	blue-black stripe	silver
Gendarmerie	blue black	silver grenade	blue black	royal blue	double stripe of blue black	silver
Garde républicaine mobile	blue black	gold grenade	blue black	royal blue	»	gold
Garde républicaine de Paris	blue black	gold grenade	red	royal blue	»	gold
Sapeurs-pompiers de la ville de Paris	black velvet	gold grenade	black velvet	dark blue	scarlet piping	gold

FORTRESS UNITS AND ENGINEERS, FRANCE, 1940

1. Fortress infantry, battle dress — 2. Beret insignia, fortress infantry — 3—5. Collar patches, known officially as *pattes de collet*: 3. Fortress units from north-eastern forts; 4. Alpine fortress units; 5. Fortress artillery — 6. Helmet insignia, fortress troops — 7. Fortress gunner — 8. Cross-section of one of the works on the Maginot Line — 9. Flag bearer, engineers — 10. Engineer's collar patch — 11. Sapeur-forestier — 12. Helmet insignia for all the preceding ranks — 13. Engineer officer in full dress

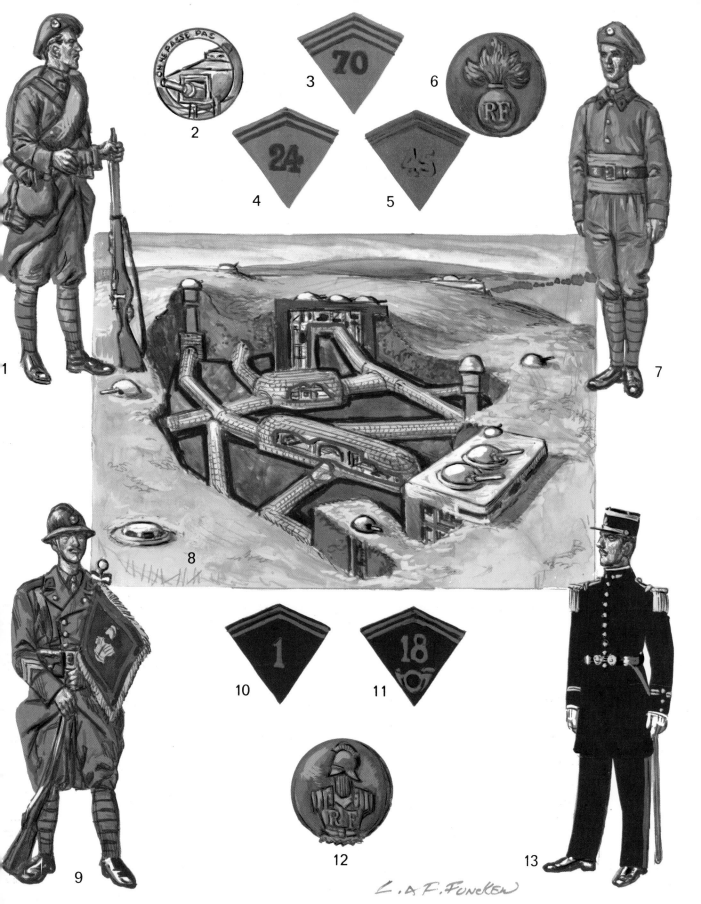

1

2

3

4

5

6

7

8

9

10

11

12

13

L. & F. Funcken

	COLLAR PATCHES	COLLAR INSIGNIA	CUFF FACINGS	TROUSERS	TROUSER STRIPES AND PIPING	BELT BUCKLE
Services						
Medical corps	blue black	gold badge	crimson velvet	red madder	blue-black stripe	gold
Pharmacists	blue black	gold badge	green velvet	red madder	blue-black stripe	gold
Dentists	blue black	gold badge	plum velvet	red madder	blue-black stripe	gold
Veterinary surgeons	blue black	silver badge	garnet velvet	red madder	blue-black stripe	silver
Commissariat	dark-blue velvet	silver badge	blue black	red madder	blue-black stripe	silver
Administration	blue black	gold badge	blue black	red madder	blue-black stripe	gold
Military justice	blue black	gold badge	black velvet	blue black	none	gold
Overseas troops						
Infantry	blue black	France: gold anchor and number; colonies: gold anchor	blue black	blue	scarlet piping	gold
Artillery	blue black	gold badge	scarlet	blue black	double stripe of scarlet	gold
Services						
Medical corps	blue black	gold badge	crimson velvet	blue	scarlet piping	gold
Pharmacists	blue black	gold badge	green velvet	blue	scarlet piping	gold
Commissariat	blue black	silver badge	blue black	blue	scarlet piping	silver
Administration	blue black	gold badge	blue black	blue	scarlet piping	gold

NORTH AFRICAN INFANTRY I

Zouaves: 1. Walking-out dress — 2. Officer in full dress. Note the open sleeve below cuffs with a fold of red silk — 3–4. Officer and soldier in battle dress — 5–8. Bottom corner of the jacket: 5. Algerian division; 6. Oran division; 7. Constantine, with detail of the regimental number on the neck opening; 8. Tunisia — 9. Helmet insignia — 10. Collar patch on battle dress

Moroccan tirailleurs: 11. Full dress with pea-jacket. Austrian knots, green colour, similar to those of pictures 7 and 17 — 12. Native sous-lieutenant — 13–14. Officers, full and battle dress (left: details of 12 and 13) — 15. Caporal in hooded cape and detail of the collar patch — 16. Battle dress (right: collar patches of the jackets of 15 and 16)

Algerian and Tunisian tirailleurs: 17. Full dress — 18. Detail of the backs — 19–22. Lower corner of jacket with distinguishing braid: 19. Algerian division; 20. Oran; 21. Constantine; 22. Tunisia — 23. Duffle-coat worn by sous-officiers and soldiers. Zouaves wore the same garment but in dark-blue material with any stripes in red — 24. Battle dress, Algerian tirailleur. Detail of the collar patch

	TYPE AND COLOUR OF UNIFORM	BUTTONS, BRAID, EPAULETTES	HEAD-DRESS	HEAD-DRESS INSIGNIA	COLLAR
École enfantine Henriot	grey-blue pea-jacket	epaulette loops	dark-blue beret	red grenade	turned down
École d'enfants de troupe	grey-blue pea-jacket	epaulette loops	red kepi, dark-blue band and braiding	red grenade	turned down
École militaire de La Flèche	dark-blue pea-jacket	epaulette loops	red kepi, dark-blue crown	red grenade	turned down
École spéciale militaire de Saint-Cyr	blue-black tunic	gold buttons, red epaulettes	sky-blue shako	yellow copper shako plate	sky blue
École polytechnique	blue-black tunic	gold epaulette fringe and buttons	cocked hat or kepi	tricolour cockade and gold gimp	stand up
École du service de santé	blue-black tunic		cocked hat or kepi with red band	gold braid on kepi	crimson velvet
École militaire d'infanterie de Saint-Maixent / École militaire d'artillerie (Poitiers) / École militaire du génie (Versailles)	*original uniform*		adjutant's kepi	gold grenade	

NORTH AFRICAN INFANTRY II

African light infantry: 1. Officer in full dress — 2. Soldier in walking-out dress with the jacket skirts worn tucked into the trousers or folded up under the belt. The enlarged collar patch was just tolerated, the regulation style not having the hunting horn — 3. Battle dress; the jacket here is worn with the skirts out

NATIVE INFANTRY

Indo-Chinese tirailleurs: 4. Battle dress and detail of the collar patch

Senegalese tirailleurs: 5. Bugler in dress worn in France — 6. Bugler in African dress — 7. Senegalese cameleer — 8. Equipment for Senegalese tirailleurs

GENERAL OFFICERS, FRANCE (*pages 24-25*)

Full dress: 1. Maréchal de France — 2. Général de corps d'armée — 3. Général de division — 4. Général de brigade — 5. Général, member of the Supreme Council of War

Walking-out dress: 6. Maréchal — 7. Général, member of the Supreme Council of War — 8. Général de division — 9. Général de brigade — 10. Général de division, in white African dress

Service dress: 11. Maréchal — 12. Général de corps d'armée — 13. Général de division — 14. Général de brigade

Working dress: 15. Général de brigade

Battle dress: 16. Maréchal — 17. Général, member of the Supreme Council of War — 18. Général de corps d'armée — 19. Général de division — 20. Général de brigade

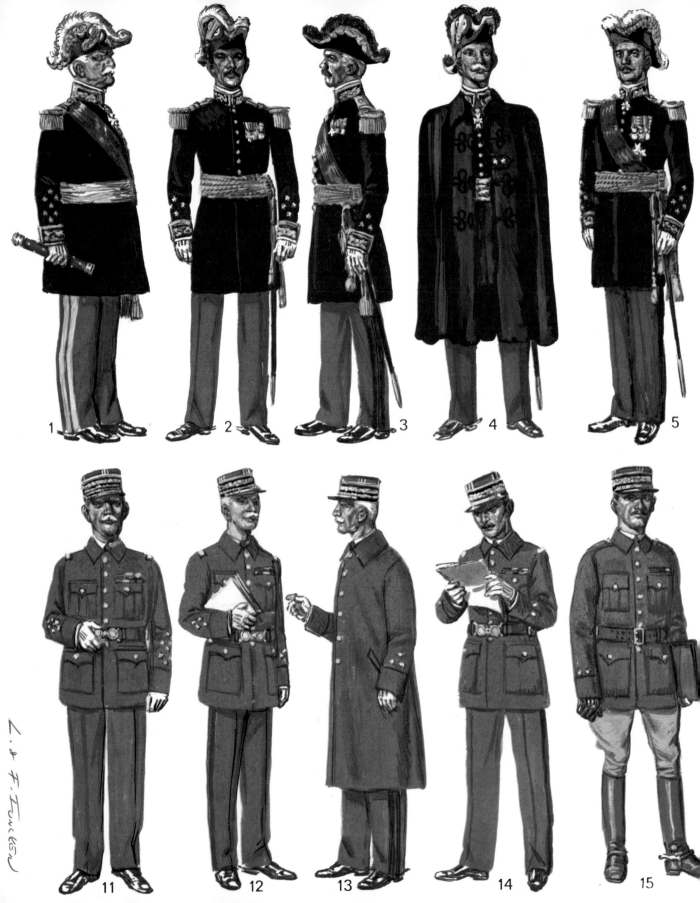

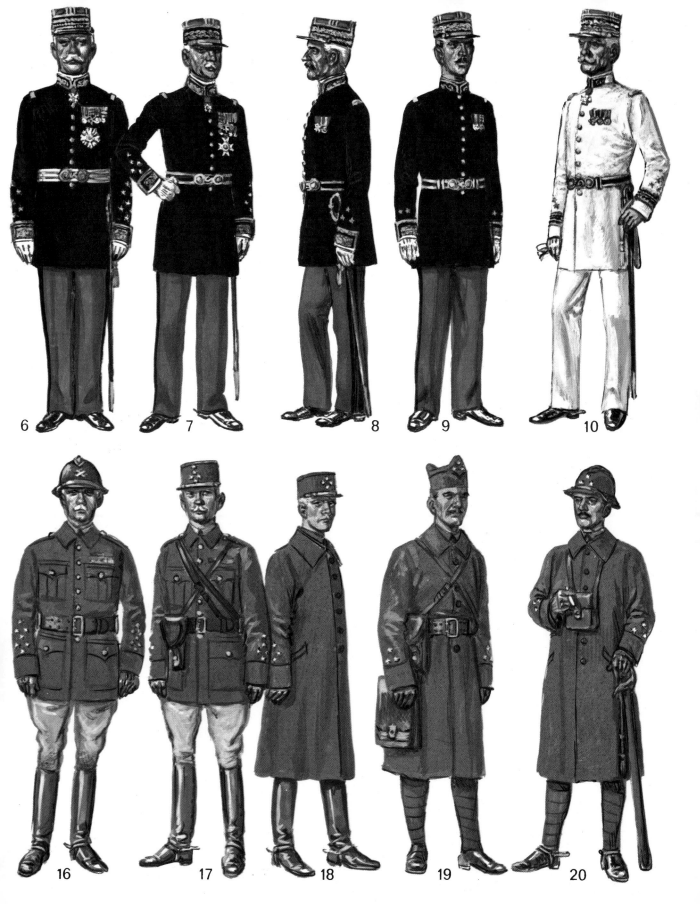

	COLLAR PATCHES	COLLAR INSIGNIA	CUFF FACINGS	TROUSERS	TROUSER STRIPES	OVERCOAT
École enfantine Henriot		red grenades		grey blue		
École d'enfants de troupe		red grenades		grey blue		grey-blue cloak
École militaire de La Flèche		red grenades		dark blue		dark-blue greatcoat
École spéciale militaire de Saint-Cyr	sky blue	yellow silk grenades[1]	sky blue	red madder	sky-blue stripe	dark blue
École polytechnique		gold grenade	blue black	blue black	double stripe of scarlet	blue black
École du service de santé	blue black	gold caduceus	crimson velvet	red	black stripes	blue black
École militaire d'infanterie de Saint-Maixent / École militaire d'artillerie (Poitiers) / École militaire du génie (Versailles)		gold grenade				original uniform

École d'application de la cavalerie (Saumur) : 1st year : original uniform; braided loop on sleeves.
2nd year : officer's uniform with red-madder trousers with double stripe and blue braid.

1 In the Ist year. In the 2nd year, gold grenades.

FOREIGN LEGION

1. Sous-officier in full dress — 2. Légionnaire in full dress — 3. Sous-officier of the cavalry regiment — 4. Infantry officer in full dress — 5. Walking-out dress for Sundays and holidays — 6. European battle dress — 7. Cavalry regiment in African battle dress — 8. Full dress — 9–10. Collar patches, cavalry

OFFICERS' DISTINCTIONS, BATTLE DRESS, 1940

	PEA-JACKET			GREATCOAT OR OVERCOAT	STRIPES	HEAD-DRESS	
	COLOUR OF COLLAR PATCH	NUMBER AND COLOUR OF BRAIDS	BADGE			TYPE AND COLOUR	BADGES
Infantry	khaki	2 dark blue	gold number	*as pea-jacket*	gold	khaki kepi	
North-eastern fortress infantry	khaki	2 dark blue	dark-blue number	»	gold	khaki beret	gold grenade
Alpine fortress infantry	khaki	3 dark blue	dark-blue number	»	gold	dark-blue beret	gold grenade
Mountain infantry	khaki	2 dark blue	dark-blue number	»	gold	dark-blue beret	gold grenade
Alpine light infantry	black	2 light-yellow silk	silver horn and number	light-blue overcoat	silver chevrons	dark-blue beret	silver hunting horn
Light infantry	black	2 light-yellow silk	silver horn and number	khaki overcoat	silver chevrons	dark-blue beret	silver hunting horn
Colonial infantry (Europeans: colonies and China)	khaki	2 scarlet	gold anchor and scarlet number	»	gold	helmet	
Colonial infantry (Europeans: France and North Africa)	khaki	2 red madder	gold anchor under red-madder number	»	gold	helmet	
Zouaves	khaki	2 red madder	gold number	»	gold	khaki chéchia[1]	narrow gold stripes
Algerian and Tunisian tirailleurs	khaki	2 light blue	gold number	»	gold	khaki chéchia	
Moroccan tirailleurs	khaki	2 light blue	gold number and star	»	gold	kepi and khaki chèche[2]	
African light infantry	khaki	2 violet	silver number	»	silver	»	
Tanks	khaki	2 light grey	silver number	»	silver	special helmet	
Cuirassiers	dark blue	2 red madder	silver number	»	silver	forage cap or helmet	
Motorised cuirassiers	dark blue	2 red madder, 1 violet	silver number	»	silver	»	
Dragoons	dark blue	2 white	silver number	»	silver	»	
Mounted dragoons	dark blue	2 white, 1 violet	silver number	»	silver	»	
Light cavalry	dark blue	2 green	silver number	»	silver	»	
Hussars	dark blue	2 sky blue	silver number	»	silver	»	
Automitrailleuses	dark blue	2 violet	silver number	»	silver	special helmet	

1 Chéchia : a soft fez-type hat worn in North Africa.
2 Chèche : a sash wrapped around the head to form a turban.

SAHARAN COMPANIES AND SPECIAL TROOPS FROM THE LEVANT

Saharan companies: 1. Officer — 2. Tirailleur — 3. Cameleer — 4. Line squadron of special troops from the Levant — 5. Tcherkesse (native horseman) cavalryman

	PEA-JACKET			GREATCOAT OR OVERCOAT	STRIPES	HEAD-DRESS	SPECIAL FEATURES
	COLOUR OF COLLAR PATCH	NUMBER AND COLOUR OF BRAIDS	BADGE				
African light infantry	dark blue	2 light yellow	silver number	»	silver	chéchia	
Algerian and Tunisian spahis	dark blue	2 light yellow	gold number	»	gold	kepi	
Moroccan spahis	dark blue	2 light yellow	gold number	khaki overcoat	gold	kepi	
Foreign Legion (cavalry)	dark blue	2 green	silver number	»	silver	kepi with khaki cover	
Reconnaissance group	dark blue	3 white	silver number	»	silver	special helmet	
Artillery	scarlet	2 dark blue	gold number	»	gold	field cap or helmet	
Artillery division of cavalry	scarlet	2 dark blue	gold number and star	»	gold		
Engineers	black velvet	2 scarlet	gold number	»	gold	»	
Baggage train	green	2 red madder	gold number	»	gold	»	
Medical corps	crimson velvet	no braid	gold number	»	gold	»	white armband with Geneva cross
Pharmacists	green velvet	»	gold badge	»	gold	»	
Medical corps administration	crimson velvet	»	gold badge	»	gold	»	
Veterinary surgeons	garnet velvet	»	silver badge	»	silver	»	
Commissariat	blue velvet	»	gold badge	»	gold	»	
Administration	khaki	»	gold badge	»	gold	»	
Military justice	black velvet	»	gold badge	»	gold	»	

ARMS AND EQUIPMENT OF THE INFANTRY

The rifle

The standard rifle used in 1939 was the 7·5 mm calibre Fusil MAS36, but many older models were also still in use, such as the Berthier Mousqueton (Carbine) models 1892 and 1916, the Berthier Fusil d'Infanterie models 1907/15 and 1916, and even the old Lebel model 1886/93.

Even the best rifle is of doubtful value in modern warfare—for the simple reason that the eye of the marksman and the cool head of the veteran are not issued with it—serving as not much more than a noisy accessory. The most that can be said for the vintage weapons mentioned above is that they were venerable; certainly they could hardly have been more

FRENCH CAVALRY I

Officers' full dress: 1. Cuirassiers — 2. Dragoons — 3. Mounted dragoons — 4. Chasseurs à cheval — 5. Hussars — 6. Automitrailleuses — 7. Remounts (identical with the Moroccan and Tunisian spahis apart from the collar patches)

Buckle plates: 8. Cuirassiers — 9. Dragoons — 10. Chasseurs à cheval — 11. Hussars

ineffective. The terrible massacres after 1914 were always effected by means of automatic weapons, mortars, and—above all—missiles from artillery and aircraft. Alongside these heavy weapons the rifle must have seemed little more effective than a catapult. The days when followers of Sergeant York[1] could imitate his exploits in battle had gone for good.

Light and heavy machine guns

The light machine gun used by the French regiments was the 1924 model, modified in 1929. With its bipod it weighed a little over 13 kilograms. It fired the 7·5 mm cartridge, and was fed by a box magazine containing 25 rounds. Heavy machine guns were the 8 mm Hotchkiss and the 7·5 mm Châtellerault, in various versions.

The grenade

The hand grenade was effective mainly as a morale booster. Its charge of cheddite and tolite was exploded after five or six seconds by a time-fused igniter.

The helmet

The regulation helmet was the 1916 *bourguignotte*, except that after 1931 it was made of manganese steel. The crown, visor and neck shield were all in one piece. The old model from the First World War was not, however, completely superseded.

Equipment

The infantryman's rucksack was divided into two parts, the upper bag which was carried on his back, and the lower bag worn on the loins. Both, as well as the haversack carried on the hip, were made of tough waterproof cloth. The three haversacks contained a wide variety of objects essential to the soldier in the field:

90 7·5 mm rounds of rifle ammunition
2 magazines, each with 25 machine-gun rounds
1 forage cap, 1 pair laced boots, 1 pair gloves
1 sweater, 1 handkerchief, 1 tie, 1 shirt, 2 pairs socks, underclothes
1 set brushes, for clothes, washing and boots

1 See vol. 1 of *Arms and Uniforms of The First World War.*

1 towel, tablet of soap
1 double tin of oil, for boots and weapons
1 special brush for weapons
1 sewing set, or 'housewife'
1 mess tin and plate, tin mug, knife, fork, spoon
1 box emergency rations containing dry biscuits, preserved meat, sugar, coffee (in tablet form), and dehydrated soup.

To this equipment must be added the 2-litre water bottle carried on the right hip, the anti-chlorine gas mask in its case, and two ammunition pouches containing a further 90 rounds of ammunition.

THE 'ENFANTS TERRIBLES' OF THE FRENCH ARMY

The reader will have noticed in the summary tables and in the illustrations one type of French army unit who, curiously, escaped the regulation khaki battle dress—the light infantrymen. Since 1921 this autonomous body had been ordered to wear khaki like all the other troops; but the *vitriers* (glaziers, nickname of the 'Chasseurs à pied') were far too attached to their traditions to accept the loss of their identity in such a monotonously impersonal colour. And indeed they made so many difficulties, provoked so much argument, and raised such vehement objections, that they finally achieved that rarest of victories, a triumph over red tape. In 1935 the Ministry of War gave the light infantry permission to leave off khaki in peacetime, though in wartime they were to continue to wear the khaki overcoat and helmet. In practice, however, the light infantry only half obeyed even this order and often wore their dark blue helmets in battle.

FRENCH CAVALRY II

1. Bugler of the dragoons, prise d'armes dress — 2. Cuirassier in combat dress — 3. Bugler of the hussars, battle dress — 4. Chasseur à cheval, battle dress — 5. Motorised reconnaissance squadron. Right, detail of the collar patch — 6. Officer of the automitrailleuses. Note the stripes of rank on the revers — 7–8. Motor cycle dragoons, driver and passenger — 9–15. Collar patches: 9. Cuirassiers; 10. Motorised cuirassiers; 11. Mounted dragoons; 12. Dragoons; 13. Hussars; 14. Chasseurs à cheval; 15. Automitrailleuses — 16. Helmet badges, motorised units and automitrailleuses

The mountain light infantry managed to escape khaki altogether and rarely used the helmet, which had anyway been discarded for many years by certain battalions.

DISTINCTIONS OF FRENCH TROOPS IN BATTLE DRESS, 1940

	PEA-JACKET			GREATCOAT OR OVERCOAT	HELMET BADGE	BERET	
	COLOUR OF COLLAR PATCH	COLOUR OF BRAID AND NUMBERS	NUMBER OF BRAIDS, BADGE			COLOUR	ORNAMENT
Infantry	khaki	blues	2	*as pea-jacket*	grenade inscribed RF	—	
North-eastern fortress infantry	khaki	blues	2	»	grenade inscribed RF	brown	casemate inscribed *'on ne passe pas'*
Alpine fortress infantry	khaki	blues	3	»	grenade inscribed RF	blue	casemate inscribed *'on ne passe pas'*
Mountain infantry	khaki	blues	2	»	grenade inscribed RF	blue	red-madder grenade
Alpine light infantry	blue	light yellow	2, a yellow horn below number	light-blue hooded cape	hunting horn inscribed RF	blue	yellow hunting horn
Light infantry	blue	light yellow	2, a yellow horn below number	khaki collar patches, 2 chevrons green numbers and horn	hunting horn inscribed RF	blue	yellow hunting horn
Colonial infantry (Europeans: colonies and China)	khaki	scarlet	2, without number, upright red anchor	*as pea-jacket*	upright anchor	—	buttons bearing an anchor
Colonial infantry (natives)	khaki	light yellow	no braids, yellow anchor	»	upright anchor	khaki chéchia (except Indo-China)	buttons bearing an anchor
Colonial infantry (Europeans: France, Levant, N. Africa)	khaki	red madder	2, red anchor under number	»	upright anchor	—	buttons bearing an anchor
Colonial infantry (natives: France, Levant, N. Africa)	khaki	light yellow	no braids, yellow anchor under number	»	upright anchor	khaki chéchia	buttons bearing an anchor

NORTH AFRICAN CAVALRY I

African light infantry: 1–2. Oriental dress — 3. Garrison and off-duty dress (identical for spahis) — 4. Lieutenant in full dress — 5. Walking-out dress with overcoat — 6. Mounted full dress — 7. Battle dress with tropical pith helmet — 8. Battle dress with Adrian helmet — 9. Collar patch for the overcoat and for the khaki battle-dress jacket — 10. Helmet insignia — 11. Detail of the shoulder strap known as the trefoil

	PEA-JACKET			GREATCOAT OR OVERCOAT	HELMET BADGE	BERET	
	COLOUR OF COLLAR PATCHES	COLOUR OF BRAID AND NUMBERS	NUMBER OF BRAIDS, BADGE			COLOUR	ORNAMENT
Zouaves	khaki	red madder	2	as pea-jacket	crescent and RF	khaki chéchia	—
Algerian and Tunisian tirailleurs	khaki	light blue	2	»	crescent and RF	khaki chéchia	—
Moroccan tirailleurs	khaki	light blue	2, star below number	»	crescent and RF	khaki chèche	—
African light infantry	khaki	violet	2	»	hunting horn inscribed RF	—	—
Foreign Legion	khaki	green	2	»	grenade inscribed RF	—	buttons, inscribed 'Légion étrangère'
Tanks	khaki	light grey	2	»	helmet and crossed cannons	blue	helmet and crossed cannons
Tank engineers	khaki	light grey	none	»	»	blue	»
Regional regiment	khaki	white braid, blue no.	1	»	»	—	—
Cuirassiers	dark blue	red madder	2	»	grenade inscribed RF	—	—
Motorised cuirassiers	dark blue	red madder, 1 violet	2 red madder, 1 violet	»	»	—	—
Dragoons	dark blue	white	2	»	»	—	—
Mounted dragoons	dark blue	white	2, white star	»	»	—	—
Light cavalry	dark blue	green	2	»	»	—	—
Hussars	dark blue	light blue	2	»	»	—	—
Automitrailleuses	dark blue	violet	2	»	Minerva's head and sun's rays	—	—
African light infantry	dark blue	light yellow	2	»	grenade inscribed RF	khaki chéchia	—
Algerian and Tunisian spahis	dark blue	light yellow	2	»	crescent and RF	khaki chéchia	—
Moroccan spahis	dark blue	light yellow	2, yellow star beneath number	»	crescent and RF	khaki chèche with white band around the base, with a coloured stripe to distinguish each squadron.	
Foreign Legion (cavalry)	dark blue	green	2, green grenade beneath number	»	grenade inscribed RF	—	buttons inscribed 'Légion étrangère'
Reconnaissance	dark blue	white	3	»	grenade inscribed RF	—	—

NORTH AFRICAN CAVALRY II

1. Algerian spahi in jacket with lower facings in the colours of the Algerian division. Above, from left to right: division from Oran, Constantine and Tunisia — 2. Algerian spahi in full prise d'armes dress — 3. Algerian spahi in walking-out dress — 4. Moroccan spahi in pea-jacket with detail of the collar patch — 5. Moroccan spahi in full dress with burnous (Arab cloak) — 6. Sous-lieutenant of the Algerian (or Tunisian) spahis in full dress with burnous — 7. Moroccan spahi captain, full dress — 8. Lieutenant of the Algerian (or Tunisian) spahis in mounted full riding dress — 9. Lieutenant of the Moroccan spahis with detail of the collar patch and the kepi insignia

NB: Only the Moroccan spahis wore the seal of Solomon, the others simply had a number.

	PEA-JACKET			CAPE OR OVERCOAT	HELMET BADGE	BERET	
	COLOUR OF COLLAR PATCHES	COLOUR OF BRAIDS AND NUMBERS	NUMBER OF BRAIDS, BADGE			COLOUR	ORNAMENT
Artillery	scarlet	blue	2	*as pea-jacket*	crossed cannons and grenade inscribed RF	—	—
Artillery division of cavalry	scarlet	blue	2, blue star beneath number	»	»	—	—
Artillery engineers	scarlet	yellow numbers	*none*	»	»	—	—
Colonial artillery (Europeans: colonies and China)	scarlet	blue	2, *no number*, blue anchor	»	upright anchor	—	buttons bearing an anchor
Colonial artillery (Europeans: France, North Africa)	scarlet	blue	2, blue anchor beneath no.	»	upright anchor	—	buttons bearing an anchor
Colonial artillery (Natives: colonies and China)	scarlet	light yellow	*none*, light-yellow anchor	»	upright anchor	khaki chéchia	—
Colonial artillery (Natives: France, North Africa)	scarlet	light yellow	*none*, light-yellow anchor beneath no.	»	upright anchor	khaki chéchia	—
Mountain artillery	scarlet	blue	2	»	crossed cannons and grenade inscribed RF	blue	scarlet grenade
Engineers	black	scarlet	2	»	breast-plate and old helmet	—	—
Sapeurs forestiers	black	scarlet	2, red hunting horn below	»	breast-plate and old helmet	—	—
Baggage train and GHQ secretaries	green	red madder	*none*	»	grenade inscribed RF	—	—
Commissariat and military administrative workers	light grey	red madder	*none*	»	grenade inscribed RF	—	—
Military nurses	red madder	light blue	*none*	»	caduceus	—	—

FLAGS AND STANDARDS

The regimental standard was the *Tricolore,* with the blue band next to the pole. It was 0·9 m square, excluding the 5 cm gold fringe, and was made of two thicknesses of silk. The obverse of the standard, with the pole to the left, had on one side the inscription in gold letters, *République française, x^e régiment d'infanterie*; on the reverse was *Honneur et Patrie* surmounting the names of the principal battles in which the regiment had fought.

The oak pole, painted blue, was topped by a gilded spearhead carrying the number and name of the regiment. A tricolour sash of silk was knotted to it bearing the same details encircled by a laurel wreath. The *fourragères*[1] and decorations awarded to particular regiments were carried on the *cravate.*

The flag was exactly like the standard, except that its dimensions were reduced to 0·6 m square.

1 *Fourragère* is a term which has no real equivalent in English; roughly it refers to the forage rope indicating the award of decorations.

NORTH AFRICAN CAVALRY III

Spahi sortie battle dress: 1. Officer (Algerian and Tunisian) — 2. Pea-jacket (Algerian and Tunisian) — 3. Walking-out dress (Moroccan spahi) — 4. Battle dress with 'gandoura' Note the wearing of the rank insignia across the chest — 5. Moroccan as 4, with fully equipped horse — 6. Algerian (or Tunisian) spahi

France at War

On Sunday, 3 September 1939, an unafraid but unenthusiastic France entered the Second World War, fulfilling its promise to come to the aid of Poland, which had been invaded by German troops. In Warsaw the news that the British and French had declared war against Germany provoked an outburst of delirious joy and soon the whole of Poland, anticipating a total reversal of the situation through Hitler being forced to fight on two fronts simultaneously, was inspired by the same wild hope.

But the powerful offensive they hoped would free them was never to come; France's military policy was defensively based, and she was not able to lead any serious attack on the borders of the Reich. The French High Command had been completely bluffed by German propaganda and the Siegfried Line was universally considered to be the formidable obstacle the Germans claimed it to be. Had not Hitler boasted on the radio of his Todt organisation, which in one year had constructed seventeen thousand impregnable fortifications on the 'Western Wall'? Indeed Hitler had described the achievement as 'one of the most remarkable of all time', and had proclaimed that no power in the world could ever succeed in breaking through the front which his engineers had constructed. In fact the enormity of these claims alone should have aroused suspicion, but the elderly strategists could remember only their experiences in the First World War and were inclined to agree with the leader of the Third Reich.

Some people did challenge these assertions, but they were promptly silenced by GHQ, who forbade even the professionals to voice their ill-omened theories publicly. The German generals heaved a massive sigh of relief when they realised that no serious attack was to threaten their Western Wall. Among these generals were some of the most illustrious of the Wehrmacht: von Manstein, Westpal, Rommel, Keitel, von Rundstedt and Jodl.

The French High Command was also taken in by another perfectly executed bluff which made them overestimate the size of the German armed forces.

According to propaganda they numbered:
- 57 active divisions
- 40 reserve divisions proper
- 35 Landwehr divisions
- 15 *Ersatztruppen*[1]

thus giving 147 infantry divisions. The number of tanks was estimated at between four and five thousand and the number of aircraft at about twelve thousand, including reserves. The reality was that at that time the Wehrmacht could command no more then ten active divisions and twelve Landwehr divisions to defend its western frontiers; forty-two active divisions were already engaged in Poland, along with all Germany's tanks and the greater part of the Luftwaffe.

Admittedly the forces available to the Allies have often been exaggerated; they were in a position to muster far fewer than the hundred divisions and eleven thousand guns which would have been needed to break through the Siegfried Line and thus change the course of history. But it is also true that in the early days of the war the Allies possessed a decided superiority of numbers in this area, and that a large-scale offensive would have produced important results.

It is true that there was the Saar offensive, which was launched on 7 September with nine divisions, and which resulted in the slow and methodical occupation of a front twenty-five kilometres long by eight wide. This offensive, much exaggerated by the press, was made without any resistance from the enemy, who

1 The three reserve groups roughly correspond to the first, second and third call-up.

ARTILLERY AND BAGGAGE TRAIN, FRANCE

1. Artillery officer in full dress — 2–4. Officer and soldiers in battle dress — 5. Artillery collar patches — 6. Collar patches for anti-aircraft artillery and spotting artillery — 7. Artillery helmet insignia (that of the baggage train carrie the grenade of the infantry) — 8. Artillery engineer — 9. Baggage train officer in full dress — 10. Battalion o artillery engineers — 11. Collar patch, equipment train

12. Machine gun M29 (Châtellerault) — 13. Offensive grenade (enlarged in relation to the guns) — 14. Sub-machine gun 1938 model — 15. MAS 1936 rifle — 16. 1886-93 model rifle — 17. 1935 model pistol

1

5

32

110

6

2

7

3

9

8

4

12

13

14

15

16

17

11

16

9

10

L. & F. Funcken

contented themselves with a similarly methodical and deliberate retreat. As they withdrew the Germans left behind them mines and booby traps, and soon the first anonymous victims of the phoney war had fallen in that so far undisputed land which lay between the Maginot and the Siegfried Lines.

The 12 September saw the collapse of the resistance of the heroic Polish army. At the same time General Gamelin produced his *Instruction personnelle numéro 4,* which pointed out the futility of attacking the Siegfried Line and ordered the Saar offensive to be stopped. The new defence line was set at such a distance from the German fortifications that it would be unable to serve as a base against an enemy counter-attack, and the memorandum added that in the event of such a counter-attack the ground must be surrendered.

Then a French communiqué of 15 September announced that a position taken on 9 September by the Germans had been recaptured. Unfortunately, however, Headquarters had not yet by this date seen fit to release the information that it had been lost! French public opinion was seriously disturbed by this, and for the first time began to have serious doubts about the objectivity of the French GHQ. At the same time the German victories in Poland were causing a great deal of comment in the Allied press. Military experts did not even bother to hide their amazement at the tactics of the German troops and extensive extracts from the book *Achtung, Panzer!* by General Guderian, which explored in depth the principles of the use of armoured vehicles, were published and knowledgeably commented on. Even so, Allied strategists reassuringly attributed the rapid victory of the German armoured divisions to the weakness of Polish resources; peace was still intact on the French front line, whatever was happening to the Poles.

On the eastern front the war had fallen into the hands of skirmishers, whose patrols attacked the enemy in one ghost village after another. In spite of their brevity, these obscure engagements often reached unparalleled levels of savagery. The novelist Guy des Cars[1] has vividly described these little-known engagements, preliminaries to the great drama of 1940.

1 In *L'Officier sans nom.*

Another war was also flaring up, far in the north of Finland,[2] a war which unexpectedly strengthened the arguments in favour of a defensive policy. The Finns had refused to accede to the territorial demands of the Russians and had succeeded in halting the Soviet forces at the fortified works of their Mannerheim Line built with the aid of Belgian officers. The Russians took three and a half months, from 30 November 1939 until 12 March 1940, to overrun Finland. Foreign observers rushed to their own conclusions: on the one hand they speculated on the mediocrity of the Russian troops, while on the other—and people drew much satisfaction from this in France—there was the remarkable effectiveness of the Mannerheim Line, which was so much smaller than the formidable chain of French fortresses.

THE MAGINOT LINE

For formidable the Maginot Line was, without a doubt. France had undertaken its construction in 1930, and the building of it had taken five years, with all of France's technical resources and three billion

2 The Finnish army is the subject of a chapter in vol. 3.

GARDE RÉPUBLICAINE ON FOOT AND HORSEBACK, GARDE MOBILE, FRANCE

Garde républicaine de Paris on toot: 1. Officer — 2. Regular sous-officier

Shoulder trefoils: 3–4. Garde and maréchal des logis-chef of the Garde républicaine mobile — 5–7. Garde républicaine de Paris, 3e, 2e, and 1re classe

Shakoes of the Garde républicaine de Paris: 8. Lieutenant-colonel — 9. Commandant — 10. Capitaine — 11. Adjudant — 12. Maréchal des logis-chef — 13. Garde

Garde républicaine mobile: 14. Officer in service dress — 15. Officer in full dress

Mounted Garde républicaine: 16. Trumpeter in full dress — 17. Detail of the back — 18. Colonel in full dress — 19. Maréchal des logis-chef in full dress

NB: Ordinary full dress did not include the plume; the corners of the tunic were not turned back, or were turned to the inside so that the red lining did not show; trousers were blue.

1 2 3 4 5 6 7 8 9 10 11 12 13 14 15 16 17 18 19

L. & F. Funcken

francs being lavished on it. The Line, 350 km long, covered the Belgian frontier to the east from the Meuse and all of the German frontier as far as Switzerland. Its main edifices were concrete blocks, 3·5 m thick by 4 m long, flush with the ground. These blocks were connected by a network of tunnels served by a small railway for the movement of troops and munitions. Built into the top of the concrete blocks were special steel turrets from which 75 or 135 guns could be fired. Each turret could also conceal a nest of machine guns, an anti-aircraft gun, a trench mortar or a search light.

These blocks, usually triangular in shape, concealed in their depths magazines, power stations and small barracks, well protected from even the most powerful bombs. Arranged in groups, and offering each other cover, they were fortifications of formidable strength. Between these monoliths there were casemates equipped with machine guns and anti-tank guns, whose carefully worked-out range of fire guaranteed a deep 'prohibited area'. No assailant would have been able to attempt to storm them without being immediately cut down by intensive gun fire from the casemates, in which troops prepared for the counter-attack were also stationed. On top of all this, in front of the first line deep anti-tank trenches and 'walls' of metal rails had been established, which armoured vehicles would be able to break through only with the greatest difficulty. Behind the forts a whole network of concrete balustrades for infantry, artillery, sound detectors, spotlights, etc. was connected to the rear by underground tunnels. These carried munitions trains at depths of 50 m and sometimes 70 m below the surface, coming up to the various chambers by means of lifts. Sound-proof and mainly air-conditioned, the barracks, offices, magazines and power stations ensured the faultless functioning of the garrison.

Still further back powerful guns on rails were ready to fire on the enemy even before he came into the range of the guns on the Line. Their mobility meant that they could be concentrated on to the point which was most threatened at any given time.

To the east there was the former defence front, comprising the old forts of Belfort, Épinal, Verdun, etc., which had been modernised, these three areas together extending to a depth of 90 to 100 km.

Throughout this gigantic and probably impenetrable conglomeration of defences there was only one weakness—the gap between the Meuse and Dunkirk. The question of who took the fatal decision not to complete the defence line is difficult to answer; certainly the members of the Supreme Council of War appear to have been convinced that the tortuous routes through the Ardennes massif constituted an insurmountable obstacle for an army of any size. Unfortunately it was at just this precise point that an army of five hundred divisions rolled through.

10 May 1940

The number of French troops in 1940 has been variously estimated, ranging from 94 to 104 divisions. On the basis of the first figure, the 94 divisions would have been as follows:

63 infantry divisions
7 motorised infantry divisions
3 cuirassier divisions
3 armoured divisions
5 cavalry divisions
13 fortress divisions.

In total, France mobilised some 2,680,000 men, of which nearly 90 per cent were occupied in defending the front from Switzerland to the sea.

GENDARMERIE AND SAPEURS-POMPIERS, FRANCE

Gendarmerie: 1. Officer in full dress — 2. Full dress, mounted — 3. Gendarme départemental in winter service dress

Gendarmerie départementale: 4. Collar — 5. Officer's cuffs — 6. Cadet officer — 7. Gendarme — 8. Regular sous-officier — 9. Gendarme's trefoil — 10. Trefoil for maréchal des logis-chef

Sapeurs-pompiers: 11. Full dress — 12. Bugler in full dress — 13. Officer's collar and cuffs — 14. Collar for sapeur with caporal-chef's sleeve — 15. Helmet

RECRUITMENT AND MILITARY SERVICE IN FRANCE

Compulsory military service had been established in France by the law of the 19th fructidor, year VI (5 September 1798). Every eligible citizen had to do his national service when reaching the age of twenty. Length of service was the same for all the forces: two years on full service, two years unattached on half pay, ten years in the first reserve, eight years in the second reserve, and finally two years in the Civil Defence. To this annual recruitment must be added the regular soldiers, who included the natives of the French colonies. Contrary to popular belief these natives were not compelled to do military service unless they were naturalised Frenchmen.

The permanent forces of the French army were divided up into:
Metropolitan forces
Overseas forces
Mobile overseas forces, stationed in France and in North Africa.

METROPOLITAN FORCES

Infantry (metropolitan)

52 infantry regiments including the alpine infantry
12 regiments of fortress infantry
26 battalions of light infantry
2 mountain battalions

Infantry (North Africa)

6 regiments of zouaves
16 regiments of Algerian tirailleurs
5 regiments of Tunisian tirailleurs
8 regiments of Moroccan tirailleurs
1 battalion of African light infantry
3 foreign regiments
5 Saharan companies, of which one was mounted

Tanks

11 tank regiments
5 armoured battalions
1 anti-tank company

Cavalry (metropolitan)

6 cuirassier regiments
12 regiments of dragoons of which one was mounted
6 regiments of light cavalry (chasseurs à cheval)
4 regiments of hussars
6 groups of cavalry machine gunners (automitrailleuses)
3 battalions of mounted dragoons
1 group of cavalry from the *École supérieure de guerre*
1 group of cavalry from the *École supérieure du génie* (engineers)

Cavalry (North Africa)

5 regiments of African light infantry
7 regiments of Algerian spahis
1 regiment of Tunisian spahis
4 regiments of Moroccan spahis
1 regiment of foreign cavalry
6 companies of remounts

Baggage Train

7 regional companies
17 metropolitan squadrons
3 Algerian squadrons
4 Moroccan squadrons
1 Tunisian squadron
1 Levantine squadron

Artillery

27 divisional horse-drawn regiments

COLONIAL INFANTRY AND ARTILLERY, FRANCE

Colonial infantry: 1. Bugler in metropolitan battle dress — 2. African dress — 3. Detail of collar — 4. Dress known as 'short' with detail of the helmet insignia — 5. White colonial dress for officers — 6. Collar patch common to all white troops in North Africa and the Levant, worn on khaki uniform — 7. Colonial infantry caporal in metropolitan town dress — 8. Colonial artillery collar patch for blue uniforms — 9. Artilleryman in metropolitan town dress — 10. Colonial artillery collar patch for khaki dress, colonies and China — 11. Colonial infantry officer in full dress — 12. Colonial artillery officer in full dress — 13. Collar patch for colonial artillery for khaki dress in North Africa, the Levant and in France — 14. Detail of trousers for 12

1

3

6

2

4

5

8

10

13

7

9

11

14

12

L. et F.
FUNCKEN

8 divisional motorised regiments
3 mountain regiments
7 foot regiments
4 horse-drawn regiments of heavy artillery
7 regiments of heavy motorised artillery
1 regiment of heavy artillery on rails
4 regiments of motorised artillery
2 artillery regiments from the horse-drawn cavalry divisions
3 artillery regiments of the motorised cavalry divisions
5 anti-aircraft artillery regiments
2 autonomous groups of artillery
10 labour battalions

Engineers

12 ordinary regiments
1 railway regiment
1 regiment of telegraphers
4 battalions of sappers
24 sections of administrative clerks
24 sections of military nurses

Gendarmerie

20 legions of departmental gendarmerie
1 legion of the gendarmerie de Paris
1 legion from Alsace-Lorraine
1 legion from Morocco
1 autonomous company from Corsica
1 company from Tunisia
1 military police establishment from the Levant
13 colonial detachments

Garde républicaine

1 legion of the Garde républicaine de Paris

Garde républicaine mobile

11 legions of the Garde républicaine mobile
1 group of Garde républicaine d'Algérie

OVERSEAS FORCES

Colonial infantry

12 regiments, battalions, or companies stationed in Morocco, in West Africa, in Guiana, in Martinique, in Guadeloupe, and in New Caledonia.

Native Infantry

17 regiments of Senegalese fusiliers
1 regiment from Chad
7 battalions of tirailleurs in West Africa
2 battalions of tirailleurs in Equatorial Africa
1 battalion of tirailleurs in French Somaliland
1 battalion of tirailleurs in the Levant
3 regiments of tirailleurs in Tonkin
1 regiment of tirailleurs in Malagasy
1 battalion of Malagasian tirailleurs
1 battalion of Cambodian tirailleurs
1 battalion of tirailleurs from the mountain dwellers of South Annam

Tanks

1 section comprising 4 companies

Colonial artillery

12 regiments
7 companies and 3 detachments of workers
3 companies and 3 detachments of motor transport

SPECIAL TROOPS FROM THE LEVANT

Infantry

8 battalions of infantry from the Levant
2 battalions of light infantry from Lebanon

Cavalry

3 line squadrons
6 Druse squadrons
8 Tcherkesse squadrons
7 squadrons from Aleppo and Djezireh

Artillery

3 special formations
These troops also had three companies of cameleers and several of machine guns.

The armoured troops and air force are discussed in more detail in the second part of this volume and in vol. 2. The navy will be the subject of a special chapter in vol. 3.

FRANCE AND THE 'LIGHTNING WAR'

Well protected behind its superb defence line in the east, the French High Command continued to ignore the many warnings offered to it by certain thoughtful young officers, and persisted in its idea of a defensive front in Belgium, the country through which it was certain Germany would sooner or later attack.

The unprotected frontier between the Meuse and Dunkirk was seen by the French as offering them a perfect opportunity for manoeuvre; it also served—so the theory ran—as a bait, for it was felt that inevitably it would tempt the Germans to invade Belgian territory, and consequently to run slap up against the French troops reinforced by the far from negligible divisions of King Leopold III. This was the firm conviction of the majority of the old generals, who remained faithful to the methods they considered sound simply because they had brought victory in 1918.

Since the end of fighting in Finland the newspapers had been starved of sensational headlines. The Second World War had once again fallen into its uncanny state of war without battles. The seas, however, were less peaceful, where German mines and submarines were beginning to make themselves feared. Then, on 13 December 1939, drama: the *Admiral Graf von Spee*,[1] a German pocket battle ship, was intercepted by the British. She sought refuge in Uruguayan waters on 14 December, and was scuttled there on 17 December.

In the air several encounters between fighters gave each of the combatants the chance to proclaim his superiority. The British 'bombarded' Berlin for the fourth time on 3 March 1940. Luminous parachute rockets preceded the scattering of leaflets and the German anti-aircraft batteries, in less light-hearted mood, destroyed one of these visiting aircraft.

1 The war at sea will be treated more fully in vol. 3.

THE WESER EXERCISE

On 9 April 1940 Hitler struck again, brutally shattering the unnatural calm. This time he invaded Norway with less than ten thousand men, a force which promptly and with remarkable efficiency strangled the Norwegian defences, over-running Denmark *en route*. This was the operation which became known as the 'Weser Exercise'.

On 10 April a communiqué from the French GHQ forecast a quiet night on the Alsace-Lorraine front and the Allied Supreme Council decided to put underway a joint operation to dislodge the Germans from their new conquest while their hold was still relatively tenuous. Between 10 and 13 April a flotilla of the Royal Navy attacked the German fleet sheltering in Narvik fjord, and by midnight of the 13th the fjord was completely cleared of the ten destroyers which were defending it, those of their crews who escaped joining the infantry of the Wehrmacht entrenched at Narvik.

This naval success encouraged the Allies into a little more daring. A British brigade and some French alpine infantry were despatched to Norway, the light infantry being part of a special unit called the *brigade de haute montagne* (high mountain brigade), which had been created on 28 February to intervene in Finland against the Soviet Union. Also with them were two battalions of the Foreign Legion which had been formed into the 13th demi-brigade with this same object. Now, one after the other, the light infantry of the 5th demi-brigade, those of the 27th who made up Colonel Béthouard's special brigade, the 13th demi-brigade of the Foreign Legion, and a Polish brigade, were posted to Great Britain, from where the Franco-British expeditionary force sailed for Norway.

Unhappily, however, the British, who had been determined from the start to be the principal engineers of the combined operation, compounded delays with technical errors to ensure the failure of the operation. The first one thousand Allied soldiers landed between 15 and 19 April with no tanks, anti-tanks guns, anti-aircraft guns or (here, perhaps, with greater justification) heavy artillery. Eight days later they were forced to carry out a hurried evacuation, an evacuation which finally demonstrated how ill-conceived the plan of attack had been.

The intervention of the French and British further north fared better, and they pulled off several successes round Narvik, the French light infantry writing one of the best pages in its military annals on the outskirts of this town. Narvik fell to the Allies on 28 May 1940, after desperate resistance from the six thousand Germans who had withstood a siege lasting six weeks. However, since 10 May 1940 the catastrophic events in France had thrown the country into chaos, and on 8 June the expeditionary corps was withdrawn from Norway, bringing with it King Haakon and the Norwegian government.

'ZERO HOUR'

'The hour of decisive battle for the German people' arrived on 10 May 1940. Simultaneously, two powerful German armies launched their attacks on Belgium and Holland: in the centre the A group of armies under von Rundstedt, in the north the B group of armies under von Beck. The C group in the south, under von Leeb, stayed under cover along the length of the Maginot Line.[1] Right from the first moments the assault manifested all the characteristics of a *Blitzkrieg*. Worked out to the last detail, 'Operation Yellow' mobilised waves of aeroplanes and armoured vehicles whose task was to open a vast highway for the German troops. Holland resisted for five days; Belgium after eighteen days went under exhausted.

The French and British, who had drawn up part of their forces along the Belgian frontier, were now called to the aid of their allies. Wheeling around Sedan the first group of armies—twenty-two French divisions—entered Belgium, where they were welcomed by the people with open arms, and installed themselves on the Dyle. Destined by the French High Command to oppose a solid front of enemy forces, these troops were made up of the best and most modern divisions France had at its disposal.

Behind the Maginot Line from Sedan to the Swiss frontier the Second and Third army corps and four armies totalling forty-three infantry divisions and ten fortress divisions made up the second group of armies. As French thinking had decided that the Ardennes

massif could not be crossed by the *Panzerdivisionen*, only thirteen divisions had been stationed in the Sedan sector, of which four were formed by the second reserve. Not a single armoured vehicle had been provided. Inevitably it was here at Sedan, axis of the first and second groups of armies and the weakest point in the French lines, that the enemy attacked. The second group was powerless against the sudden assault of von Kleist's armoured vehicles, seven divisions strong and accompanied by three motorised divisions and eighteen infantry divisions.

This awe-inspiring army, which was further reinforced by units of the Sixteenth German army, in three days opened a gap sixty kilometres wide between Sedan and Namur; General von Rundstedt, commanding the A group of armies, did not hesitate to send his armoured vehicles through the breach before the French could regroup.

On 21 May 1940 the victorious German tanks reached Abbeville, surrounding the British Expeditionary Forces, the First and Sixth French armies, and the whole of the Belgian army in Flanders. For the Anglo-French, now cut off from their base, there remained only one escape route, the sea; the four hundred thousand men who retreated to Dunkirk withstood the bombardment like lions, thus enabling 337,000 of their number to escape to England.

From outside this noose the French High Command tried desperately to break the German stranglehold, but apart from a counter-attack led by the tanks of a certain Colonel de Gaulle, nothing serious could be attempted. Nor did the retirement of fifteen generals, or the efforts of General Weygand—who planned to rebuild a defence line on the Somme and on the Aisne—stem the tide of the re-formed divisions of the Wehrmacht. Several spearheads of French soldiers attempted to oppose the German advance, and were cut down where they stood.[2] Among these unknown young heroes, all too often unremembered, were pupils from the cadet school at Saumur, who sacrificed themselves unstintingly to create a last glow of glory before France disappeared into the twilight.[3]

1 For details of the German forces, see pp. 68-80.

2 French losses rose to a total of ninety-two thousand killed.
3 The German commander praised without reservation the heroism of these cadets; in Germany the newspapers *Der Vormarsch* and *Deutsche Allgemeine Zeitung* also paid tribute to these pupils from Saumur.

Germany and Hitler

The future master of the Third Reich, Adolf Hitler, was born near Braunau am Inn in Austria on 20 April 1889. His father, Alois, was an unimportant customs official who had changed his maternal name of Schicklgruber for Hitler, without any suspicion of the notoriety this name was later to achieve. The young Adolf spent his first sixteen years in the area of Linz. At the end of a secondary education in which he in no way distinguished himself, he decided to take up painting as a career; and after the loss of his father in 1903 and his mother in 1908 Adolf—provided with a small allowance from his mother's estate—set off to try his luck in Vienna, sitting the entrance examination for the School of Fine Arts there, but without success. Still determined to live by his art, the young man began painting postcards for a living, but inevitably this somewhat unrealistic plan fell through, and in order to survive he took a job as a skilled labourer for a building company, this time redirecting his artistic ambitions towards architecture.

At the outbreak of the First World War Hitler was in Munich, where he had settled after being declared unfit for military service in Austria—a fact which did not prevent him from enlisting as a volunteer in the Bavarian infantry, in the 16th 'List' regiment of the reserves. Hitler was to spend four years at the front, employed as a runner by his HQ, and by 1918 had reached the rank of corporal. He was also decorated twice—with the iron cross second-class (1914), and the iron cross first-class (1918); a rare distinction for the rank. In spite of these decorations, however, as an unknown corporal it would have seemed absurd to have thought of him as heading for the exceptional destiny which was in fact his. Perhaps those hard years had strengthened Hitler; and more importantly, perhaps, they had rekindled his belief in himself, disheartened as he had been by the frustrations and humiliations of his civilian life before the war.

Hitler was deeply affronted by the punitive clauses of the Treaty of Versailles, and soon he was immersed in what were essentially political activities. In the role of special agent for the army, he began to preach hatred of pacifism, all the time observing at close quarters the activities of the many small parties which were springing up in a Germany now torn apart by revolution and economic chaos.

It was during this period of his life that Hitler came across a minute party—the German Workers Party—although with 7·50 marks in the kitty and only six members it would have been better described as a club. He enrolled in September 1919, becoming its seventh member. In 1920 the future master of Germany took control of this tiny party, renaming it *Nationalsozialistische Deutsche Arbeiter Partei*—NSDAP—better known as the *Nazi Partei*. Thus Hitler became the uncontested chief of a movement which he had been in from the beginning, and which was already enjoying considerable notoriety.

The party's fundamental ideology was simple: to sweep aside liberal and democratic principles in order to promote a fanatical and exclusive nationalism in the working-class masses. Nazism had been born, though less spontaneously than one might think, for Hitler had long before been indoctrinated by certain Austrian precursors. There was Lueger, for instance, with his anti-capitalist and anti-semitic Christian Socialist Movement, and von Schönerer, that fierce partisan of a united German expansionist policy against the Habsburgs. And in fact it had been a disciple of von Schönerer, Karl Hermann Wolf, who had founded the tiny German Workers Party which Hitler was to inherit.

The rapid acceptance of the NSDAP in Bavaria led Hitler to attempt to seize power by a 'putsch', which he pushed through on 9 November 1923. The affair turned out disastrously. Although he was supported by three thousand men of the *Sturmabteilungen* (SA) and the *Schutzstaffeln* (SS) the Nazis were dispersed by the police, leaving sixteen dead on the pavement. Hitler was arrested and sentenced to five years imprisonment, and the SA and SS were banned. However, the attempted 'putsch' was not totally disastrous for Hitler: it secured him enormous publicity, while at the same time convincing him that only ostensibly legal means would assure success for his party.

Hitler's imprisonment did not last long; it was in the fairly comfortable prison of Landsberg, and it was here that he wrote the first volume of *Mein Kampf*. Out of his failed 'putsch' Hitler was later to make one of the great moments of Nazi history, and to create for the most loyal of his followers the decoration of 9 November, called the *Blutorden* or Blood Order.

The years which followed, bringing the spectacular recovery of the German economy, calmed the formerly ardent working-class revolutionaries; better fed and relatively prosperous, they became noticeably cooler to the call of National Socialism. It was in response to this changed situation that the Nazi leader, with rare mental dexterity, applied himself to conquering a now more receptive public, the middle classes who had been ruined by inflation. As party funds were by now seriously depleted, he squeezed financial aid from the rich by dangling before their eyes the spectre of Communism, over which he swore to triumph; it was a promise which found an instantaneous response from his new audience. From 27,000 in 1925, the number of NSDAP followers rose to 108,000 in 1928, and to 178,000 in 1929.

The terrible economic crisis which hit the world in that year, reaching its peak in 1932, only strengthened the Nazi Party's position, to the great detriment of all the other traditional parties with the exception of the Communists. The July elections of 1932 gave Hitler 37 per cent of the total vote. This was good, but not good enough for Adolf Hitler, who wanted absolute power. He accepted the post of Chancellor of the Reich in a coalition government, but only because he both knew and intended the situation to be a transitional one. New elections were fixed for 5 March 1933 and the Nazis moved determinedly into the attack. The Reichstag was burned down, an act which was blamed on the Communists, and which unleashed against them a wave of merciless persecution; the Communist Party was declared illegal and its leaders arrested or beaten up. The elections showed the effects of all this, for 44 per cent of the poll now went to Hitler's party. And since the seats which had been gained by the Communists in spite of their newly declared illegality were to remain empty, this result was in fact equivalent to an absolute majority. German democracy had received a mortal blow.

Now that Hitler had eliminated the other parties,

allies and rivals, suppressed all opposition, and reduced the Church to impotence, his next task was to bring some order to his own party, particularly among the SA, who were drifting more and more in the direction of becoming a leftist breakaway group under the leadership of their chief, Ernst Röhm, one of Hitler's earliest associates. It was necessary to strike swiftly and fiercely. On 30 June 1934 the soldiers of the *Schutzstaffeln* ('protection squads'), the SS, Hitler's personal bodyguard, led by their *Reichsführer* Heinrich Himmler, proceeded with their bloody purge. Röhm, his second-in-command Edmund Heines, and many other members of the SA were executed without trial. Other adversaries of Hitler, Gregor Strasser and Schleicher among them, also disappeared that night—the night which later came to be known as 'the night of the long knives'.

PARAMILITARY NAZI ORGANISATIONS
Nationalsozialistische Deutsche Arbeiter Partei — NSDAP (Nazi Party), 1940 I

Collar patches for the subdivisions: 1. District — *Gauleitung* — 2. Circle — *Kreisleitung* — 3. Local Group — *Ortsgruppe*. These three groups were covered by the *Reichsleitung*, recognisable by the carmine collar patch shown in the four columns on the left. The common ranks in the four subdivisions are superimposed — 4. Politischer Leiter non-party member — 5. Politischer Leiter party member — 6. Helfer — 7. Oberhelfer — 8. Arbeitsleiter — 9. Ober-Arbeitsleiter — 10. Haupt-Arbeitsleiter — 11. Bereitschaftsleiter — 12. Ober-Bereitschaftsleiter — 13. Haupt-Bereitschaftsleiter — 14. Einsatzleiter — 15. Ober-Einsatzleiter — 16. Haupt-Einsatzleiter — 17. Gemeinschaftsleiter — 18. Ober-Gemeinschaftsleiter — 19. Haupt-Gemeinschaftsleiter — 20. Abschnittsleiter — 21. Ober-Abschnittsleiter — 22. Haupt-Abschnittsleiter — 23. Bereichsleiter — 24. Ober-Bereichsleiter — 25. Haupt-Bereichsleiter — 26. Dienstleiter — 27. Ober-Dienstleiter — 28. Haupt-Dienstleiter — 29. Befehlleiter — 30. Ober-Befehlleiter — 31. Haupt-Befehlleiter — 32. Reichsleiter — 33. Gauleiter

The lower subdivisions had a system of ranks which became simpler lower down the scale. Thus the *Gauleitung* went from Ober-Befehlleiter, fig. 30, to the rank of Gauleiter, fig. 33, with all grades on a bright red ground. The *Kreisleitung* with its black ground only went up to the rank of Dienstleiter, fig. 26. The *Ortsgruppe*, with pale brown ground, did not go above the rank of Ober-Abschnittsleiter, fig. 21.

34. Helfer from an *Ortsgruppe* in overcoat and in marching uniform — 35. Abschnittsleiter from a *Gauleitung* in overcoat with open revers — 36. Pack — 37. Bread bag and water bottle

The final obstacle in Hitler's way, the ageing Field Marshal Hindenburg, died on 2 August 1934. From this date on Hitler abolished the presidency, taking over all its powers as *Führer* and *Reichskanzler,* that is 'guide and chancellor of the Reich'. The referendum of 19 August 1934 was called to establish the backing of the German people for Hitler; he polled 88·2 per cent of the votes. So Adolf Hitler was now the Führer of eighty million people. His next task was to become the *generalissimo* of the battles to come, through which a 'new order' would be created in Europe.

HITLER'S PARAMILITARY ORGANISATIONS

The NSDAP

Leafing through the *Organisationbuch* of the NSDAP one cannot help being impressed by the extraordinary attention to detail which went into its preparation. (The plates in this book illustrating the uniforms of the various Nazi groups are taken from it.) Even though the uniforms shown constitute a relatively complete picture of the military aspects of Nazism, it is not possible in the confines of four volumes, to reproduce even one-tenth of the badges, insignia, lance pennons and flags which adorned and distinguished the various echelons of each group—groups which in themselves were extremely varied and hierarchical.

The most notable group, both in numbers and for the importance of its functions, was the NSDAP. Here we shall restrict ourselves to reproducing the paper entitled 'Organisation of the Party', which was published during the war in the celebrated review *Signal*:

The Party Organisation was born out of the practical needs resulting from its military role, but right from the outset this organisation has been directed towards the ideal of the 'Party State' and also towards the ideal of employing each individual for the good of all, which must be for his own good too. The smallest unit is the *Block* (block), followed in order of size by the *Zelle* (cell), the *Ortsgruppe* (local group), the *Kreis* (circle), and the *Gau* (district).

The first unit, the block, is made up of the family the cell is made up of the inhabitants of up to several streets; the local group covers entire neighbourhoods—in towns whole districts; the typical size of the circle is a medium-sized town of about 250,000 inhabitants; the district takes in a number of towns and villages in a given area.

Because of its size, the *Gau* corresponds to a province, and in the Reich there is many a *Gau* which both in area and in population exceeds some of the smaller European states. The *Gau* is by far the largest administrative unit in the Party Organisation. The initiative which comes from the central government of the Reich flows directly into the *Gau*. This political will can be likened to an electric current, which enters the *Gau* and is dispersed through the various circles dependent on it.

In their turn the circles direct the current to the local groups and cells. Here the wires split again channelling the current into the 'blocks' of individual families, with the final result that each citizen of a population of eighty million finds himself connected to the central director's office. The whole network is organised in such a manner that any short-circuit is automatically picked up at the nearest centre and can be reported to the Reich government.

This system of organising the Party is both solid and simple enough to make use of all those facets of political life which are essential to the life of a great

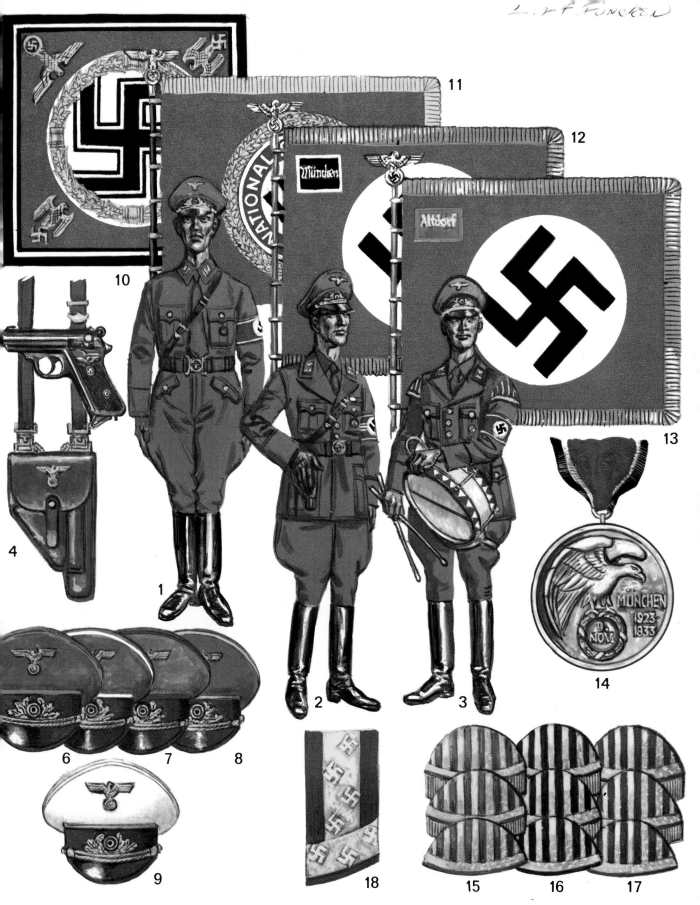

L. & F. Funcken

1 2 3 4 6 7 8 9 10 11 12 13 14 15 16 17 18

München

Altdorf

AM MÜNCHEN
9 NOV 1923-1933

people, while at the same time instilling a new sense of purpose into all the vital areas of the nation. It is a system which will result in the realisation of all the tasks imposed upon the Party; all the creative activities concerning, for example, public health, the education of the young, and social assistance for the worker (notably the improvement of working conditions, the provision of recreation centres, the question of holidays, salaries, etc.). All the precious revolutionary and ideological life-blood, which must be transmitted to the professions, to industry, to commerce, and to the peasant population, passes through the channels of the Party Organisation. As a footnote, one must add that on top of all this the system had the inestimable advantage of being able to suppress any idea which was in the least subversive or likely to interfere with its smooth working!

NSDAP uniforms

As the illustrations show, uniforms did not vary between the different subdivisions of the NSDAP, apart from the colour of the patches on the collar and the piping on the cap and collar. In each subdivision rank was distinguished by the gold insignia shown in the illustrations and also by the decoration on the brassards worn on the left arm. These brassards were ornamented with gold laurel wreaths, and these increased in number according to rank. The *Ortsgruppe* had nine different types. The *Politische Leiter* ('political leaders') had the right to an honorary weapon—*Ehrenwaffe*—an automatic 7·65 mm calibre PPK Walther.

The Jungvolk

The *Jungvolk* (Young People) was a movement which recruited all children called *Pimpfe*, from the age of ten, and prepared them for entry into the Hitler Youth.

The Hitler-Jugend

The Hitler Youth took in boys from fourteen to eighteen. The organisation possessed a naval branch with its own Naval College and a small flotilla.

The Reichsarbeitsdienst

'National Labour Service' was compulsory for all adolescents of both sexes for a period of twelve months, for the boys prior to military service.

The Sturmabteilungen der NSDAP (SA)

As we have already noted, the SA were the strong-arm section of the Nazi Party. All volunteers, the men served in the organisation between the ages of eighteen and forty-five. Their importance declined drastically after 1934.

The Schutzstaffeln (SS)

The SS were an elite recruited mainly from party members. From 1929 strict regulations governed their lives; for example they could only marry women who were able to prove the purity of their Aryan blood for at least two centuries. By 1939 they numbered

PARAMILITARY NAZI ORGANISATIONS
The Sturmabteilungen of the NSDAP or SA

1. Obertruppführer in full service dress — 2. Standartenführer, undress — 3. Rottenführer in overcoat

Kepis: 4. Standartenführer — 5. Stabschef

Shoulder straps: 6. Ordinary SA-Mann to Obertruppführer — 7. Sturmführer to Sturmhauptführer — 8. Sturmbannführer to Standartenführer — 9. Obertruppführer to Obergruppenführer — 10. Stabschef

Collar patches: 11. SA-Mann — 12. Sturmmann — 13. Rottenführer — 14. Scharführer — 15. Oberscharführer — 16. Truppführer — 17. Obertruppführer — 18. Sturmführer — 19. Obersturmführer — 20. Sturmhauptführer — 21. Sturmbannführer — 22. Obersturmbannführer — 23. Standartenführer — 24. Oberführer — 25. Brigadeführer — 26. Gruppenführer — 27. Obergruppenführer — 28. Stabschef

29. SA dagger — 30. Regional standard (Munich) — 31. Flag of a Sturm or assault formation (from the verb 'stürmen', 'to make an assault'). The gold or silver fringes of these flags varied according to the colour of the button worn by the various regional groups, which were further distinguished by the colour of their collar patches. Although they look obscure, the inscriptions on the collar patches were quite clear to the initiated. For example, in fig. 11 the 32/L signifies 32nd Sturm of the Leibstandarte, a bodyguard unit. The 33/1 of fig. 12 means 33rd Sturm of the Standarte 1, or regiment 1. The letter J stands for Jägerstandarte, or light infantry regiment. The main regions were distinguished by the following colours: Westphalia, claret; Brandenburg, black; Thuringia, apple green; Saxony, dark green; Silesia, sulphur yellow; Bavaria, light blue.

München

DEUTSCHLAND
ERWACHE

11   12   13
14   15   16
17
18
19
20
21
22
23
24
25
26
27
28

30

31

1   2   3

6   7   8   9   10

L. & F. FUNCKEN

240,000, and were seen as a 'reincarnation' of the old order of Teutonic knights. They finally became independent of the SA after the famous night of 30 June 1934. Their uniforms after 1940 are discussed in a later volume.

The Nationalsozialistische Kraftfahr-Korps (NSKK)

The 'national socialist motor vehicle corps' was a motorised unit which existed alongside the fighting sections of the army as an independent organisation.

The Nationalsozialistische Fliegerkorps (NSFK)

The members of this flying corps trained German youths in the practicalities of gliding, in this way nurturing the future pilots of the Luftwaffe.

The Diktat Army

This was the name given to the small Reichswehr army, which had been reduced to one hundred thousand men by one of the clauses in the Treaty of Versailles. The word 'Diktat' owed its popularity and subsequent adoption into the language to the vigour with which it expressed the hostility and indignation of the German people towards a treaty which they felt had been imposed upon them and which they knew to be dishonourable. If the Treaty of Versailles was harsh

PARAMILITARY NAZI ORGANISATIONS
Hitler-Jugend (Hitler Youth)
Reichsarbeitsdienst (National Labour Service)
Nationalsozialistisches Fliegerkorps (National Socialist Flying Corps)

Hitler Youth:
1. Scharführer, summer marching dress — 2. Bannführer, service dress — 3. Member of the Deutsches Jungvolk. Shoulder straps: 4. Hitlerjunge — 5. Rottenführer — 6. Oberrottenführer — 7. Kameradschaftsführer — 8. Ober-Kameradschaftsführer — 9. Scharführer — 10. Oberscharführer — 11. Gefolgschaftsführer — 12. Obergefolgschaftsführer — 13. Hauptgefolgschaftsführer — 14. Stammführer — 15. Oberstammführer — 16. Bannführer — 17. Oberbannführer — 18. Hauptbannführer — 19. Gebietsführer — 20. Obergebietsführer — 21. Stabsführer — 22. Dagger of the Hitler-Jugend — 23. Leader's dagger, carried only under special authorization — 24. Flag of the 33rd Bann of the Hitler Youth

Arbeitsdienst:
25. Arbeitsmann — 26. Abteilung or section flag

Shoulder straps: 27. Arbeitsmann — 28. Arbeitsmann volunteer, first class — 29. Vormann — 30. Obervormann — 31. Truppführer — 32. Obertruppführer — 33. Unterfeldmeister — 34. Feldmeister — 35. Oberfeldmeister — 36. Oberstfeldmeister — 37. Arbeitsführer — 38. Oberarbeitsführer — 39. Oberstarbeitsführer — 40. Generalarbeitsführer — 41. Ober-Generalarbeitsführer — 41b. Reichsarbeitsführer — 42-46. Arm insignia for subdivisions — 47. Reichsarbeitsdienst dagger

Fliegerkorps:
48. Obersturmbannführer, undress

Ranks: 49 NSFK-Mann — 50. Sturmmann — 51. Rottenführer — 52. Scharführer — 53. Oberscharführer — 54. Truppführer — 55. Obertruppführer — 56. Sturmführer — 57. Obersturmführer — 58. Sturmhauptführer — 59. Sturmbannführer — 60. Obersturmbannführer — 61. Standartenführer — 62. Oberführer — 63. Brigadeführer — 64. Gruppenführer — 65. Obergruppenführer — 66. Korpsführer — 67. Fliegerkorps dagger

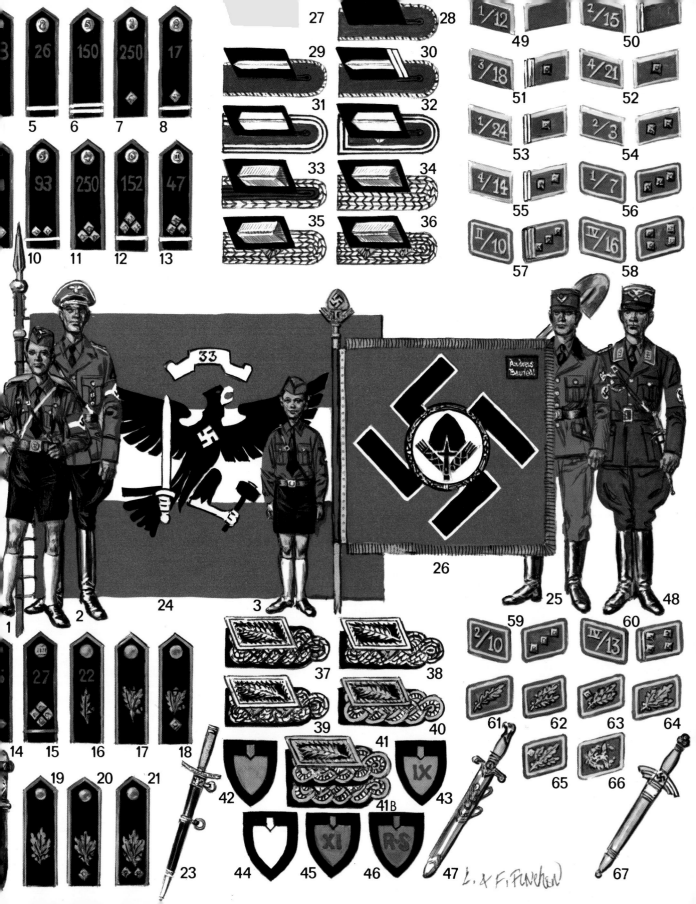

in the political arrangements it dictated, it was positively draconian on economic matters and Germany was constantly a prey to crisis, inflation and unemployment. The refusal of the moratorium begged for by the Germans, and the occupation of the Ruhr in 1923 by the French and Belgians by way of security, only served to inflame German nationalism. The army too had been able to avoid facing up to the reality of defeat. At the same time they could shift responsibility for the Compiègne armistice by having it signed by a civilian, Erzberger, and the heads of General Headquarters had soon convinced the people that defeat had come about solely through the treachery of the politicians. Indeed most of them had convinced themselves of this convenient version of the facts.

The man in charge of this new army was General Hans von Seeckt, and he was the perfect choice, a man who combined an utterly sound knowledge of his profession with a penetrating intelligence and a deep understanding of men. To begin with, the impoverished Reichswehr, with its four thousand officers and ninety-six thousand men, deprived of guns of more than 10·5 cm calibre, with no armoured vehicles or aircraft, and with a navy of fifteen thousand men and eighteen warships of limited tonnage, was the laughing stock of the world. The soldiers too were compelled to sign up for a period of twelve years, a long-term volunteer system imposed by the Treaty of Versailles which was supposed to prevent the training of large numbers of men such as could happen in a conscripted army with shorter periods of service.

PARAMILITARY NAZI ORGANISATIONS
Allgemeine Schutzstaffeln der NSDAP (SS) and SS-Verfügungstruppen (SS-VT), 1932-1940 (Pages 62-63)

1. First SS uniform worn until 1936. SS-Unterscharführer — 2. Black uniform introduced in 1932. The SS-Oberscharführer wears the old-style soft cap; here, the service and parade dress is shown — 3. Rottenführer in overcoat with the later stiffened cap for soldiers and NCOs of the SS — 4. Field service dress for an SS-VT soldier (SS-Verfügungstruppen, troops at disposal), the forerunners of the Waffen-SS — 5. SS-Sturmbannführer in raincoat — 6. Oberführer in full dress. Behind the first three figures is the flag of the first SS-Standarte 'Julius Schreck' — 7. (left) Chevron of honour awarded to pre-1933 SS men; and (right) chevron of honour awarded to ex-soldiers and policemen who were members of the SS before 1933

Shoulder straps: 8. SS-Mann to Hauptscharführer — 9. Untersturmführer to Hauptsturmführer — 10. Sturmbannführer to Standartenführer — 11. Oberführer to Obergruppenführer — 12. Reichsführer SS, special shoulder strap — 13. Leibstandarte SS Adolf Hitler — 14. SS-Standarte (regiment) 1 Deutschland — 15. SS-Standarte (regiment) 2 Germania — 16. Arm insignia, official of the SS Race and Settlement Department — 17. Cap insignia — 18. Cap insignia — 19. Officer's belt buckle — 20. Belt buckle, other ranks — 21. Dagger, 1933 — 22. Dagger, 1936 — 23. Sleeveband for Leibstandarte SS Adolf Hitler — 24. Sleeveband for Allgemeine SS-Standarte 59 named after Wilhelm Loeper.

Ranks: 25. SS-Mann — 26. Sturmmann — 27. Rottenführer — 28. Unterscharführer — 29. Scharführer — 30. Oberscharführer — 31. Hauptscharführer — 32. Untersturmführer — 33. Obersturmführer — 34. Hauptsturmführer — 35. Sturmbannführer — 36. Obersturmbannführer — 37. Standartenführer — 38. Oberführer

— 39. Brigadeführer — 40. Gruppenführer — 41. Obergruppenführer — 42. Reichsführer. The collar patches worn on the right side of the collar bore the SS insignia peculiar to the unit (see above).

Special collar patches: 43. Leibstandarte SS Adolf Hitler — 44. SS-Standarte 1 Deutschland (VT) — 45. SS-Standarte 2 Germania (VT) — 46. SS Totenkopfverbande (SS-VT).

PARAMILITARY NAZI ORGANISATIONS
Nationalsozialistisches Kraftfahr-Korps, NSKK

1. Scharführer, college dress — 2. NSKK-Mann, full service dress — 3-4. Sturmführer and Rottenführer, river-tug units, service dress — 5. NSKK kepi, all ranks up to Obertruppführer. The edelweiss on the side denotes an alpine unit — 6. Kepi, Sturmführer attached to the corps directorate — 7. Aiguillette, adjutant of the Korps Führung (High Command)

Shoulder straps: 8. NSKK-Mann to Obertruppführer — 9. Sturmführer to Sturmhauptführer — 10. Staffelführer to Standartenführer — 11. Oberführer — 12. Brigadeführer to Obergruppenführer — 13. Korpsführer

Ranks: 14. NSKK-Mann — 15. Sturmmann — 16. Rottenführer — 17. Scharführer — 18. Oberscharführer — 19. Truppführer — 20. Obertruppführer — 21. Scharführer — 22. Obersturmführer — 23. Sturmhauptführer — 24. Staffelführer — 25. Oberstaffelführer — 26. Standartenführer — 27. Oberführer — 28. Brigadeführer — 29. Gruppenführer — 30. Obergruppenführer — 31. Korpsführer. The figures and letters served the same purpose as in the other organisations. The first figure indicated the number of the Sturm, the letter M Motorstandarte, and the following numerals the number of the regiment.

32–33. Regimental standard and pennon of a Sturm

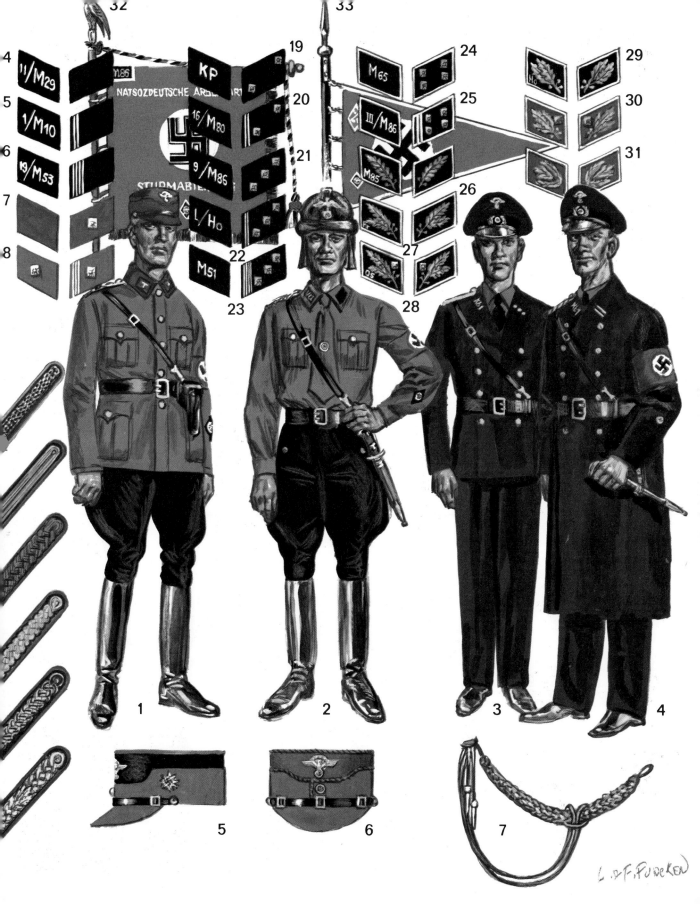

32

33

34

35

31

30

29

28

27

26

25

7

8   9   10   11   12   13   14   15

1   2   3

L. & F. FUNCKEN

In spite of all this, the German were firmly resolved to re-form their army in as little time as possible, and they made of their hundred thousand men a hothouse for future officers and NCOs. Right from the outset the Reichswehr had forty thousand NCOs to fifty-six thousand men. And the organisers of the Wehrmacht, by ruthlessly rejecting all outdated theories and equipment, showed that they knew how to profit from the situation of having to start again from nothing. The meagrest of available materials were put to use in trying out new tactics. Tanks, which were forbidden, were replaced on manoeuvres by cars covered in wood and fabric panels in imitation of armour plate. Abroad they were the cause of much hilarity, and more than one foreign newspaper printed photographs of these poor rickety caricatures of tanks, along with some caustic comment, with no understanding at all of the fierce will and consequent terrible menace concealed behind the *Tankattrappen*. Nor were foreign observers aware of the fact that as a result of a secret agreement a test centre for German tank engineers had been in operation in Kazan in Soviet territory since 1926.

The indefatigable von Seeckt had soon contacted and assembled all the patriotic members of former fighting units, such as the *Stahlhelm*, the 'steel helmets', its cadet section the *Jungstahlhelm*, and the *Arbeitskommandos*, known sometimes as the black Reichswehr. By 1930 the Reichswehr still showed its hundred thousand men, but behind it were ranged two hundred thousand trained reserves, in addition to the impressive potential of the police forces, the *Stahlhelm*, and numerous members of the various wings of the National Socialist Party. Five years later, the Wehrmacht was to sign its pact of blood and suffering with Hitler.

Austria and the Anschluss

Under the terms of the Treaty of Saint-Germain, dictated to them by their conquerors, the Austrian army was not allowed to exceed thirty thousand men and, like Germany, had to rely on long-term (twelve-year) volunteers. Himself Austrian by birth, Adolf Hitler bitterly resented these strictures and since 1936 had been planning an invasion of Austria to carry out his *Anschluss*, the annexation he had dreamed of for so long. This projected invasion, known as 'Operation Otto', raised the strongest objections in the German army HQ, which considered that the troops were still not sufficiently organised to attempt such a move. The generals in opposition to the plan were promptly dismissed, to be replaced by two more docile officers, Wilhelm Keitel and Alfred Jodl—names which were to achieve great fame and notoriety in later years.

GERMAN ARMY BEFORE THE HITLER REGIME

1–2. Senior officers — 3–4. Soldier — 5. Leutnant — 6. Cavalryman — 7. Alpine infantry — 8. Tank personnel with section of imitation tank — 9. Sailor — 10. Armoured car — 11. 1916 model helmet — 12. 1918 model helmet sometimes called 'The cavalry model' — 13. For comparison, 1935 model helmet of the Third Reich

Ranks — arm insignia: 14. Oberschütze (Oberreiter in the cavalry) — 15. Gefreite — 16. Obergefreite — 17. Stabsgefreite
Shoulder straps: 18. Unteroffizieranwärter (acting NCO) — 19. Unteroffizier — 20. Unterfeldwebel (Unterwachtmeister in the cavalry) — 21. Feldwebel (Wachtmeister in the cavalry) — 22. Oberfeldwebel (Oberwachtmeister in the cavalry) — 23. Leutnant — 24. Oberleutnant — 25. Hauptmann (Rittmeister in the cavalry) — 26. Major — 27. Oberstleutnant — 28. Oberst — 29. Generalmajor — 30. Generalleutnant — 31. General — 32. Oberstabsartz (major-doctor) — 33. Generalstabsveterinär — 34. Ministerialdirektor — 35. Armeemusikinspizient (inspector of military music)

The arms of service appeared on the shoulder strap piping up to the rank of Oberst (colonel). For the infantry it was white; light infantry, green; cavalry, yellow; artillery, bright red; engineers, black; transport corps, pink; signals, light brown, and later lemon yellow. The translations of the above ranks are given in the text.

His hands no longer tied by his generals, Hitler was now ready to 'fly to the aid of a people in spirit German and persecuted in Austria'. He had already extracted harsh concessions from the Austrian government in February 1938 and now, on 11 March, he issued Austria with an ultimatum, in which he demanded 'the unconditional surrender of the oppressors of the people', that is to say the dismissal of Chancellor Schuschnigg.

In his attempts to resist Hitler the Austrian chancellor had sought to obtain the support of the powers that had set up the new Austria, but France would go no further than to instruct her ambassador in Berlin to protest in the strongest possible terms; Great Britain did likewise. As for fascist Italy, it was useless to turn to her. True, not so long ago she had shown herself to be Austria's most reliable protector; a few years earlier she had not hesitated to mass her forces on the Brenner to foil the *Anschluss*. But times had changed. Had not the end of 1936 marked the birth of the 'Rome-Berlin Axis'? So when at the last moment Hitler made Mussolini a party to his intentions, Mussolini assured him of his full support.

In Vienna this brought collapse. Schuschnigg, who could no longer count on any support, resigned and President Miklas was forced to ask the Austrian National Socialist, Seyss-Inquart, to form a new government. Without further delay, Seyss-Inquart broadcast an appeal from the radio station at Vienna in which he called upon the German troops to come and maintain order in Austria, united in brotherhood with Austrian SA units. In the streets of Vienna and throughout Austria spontaneous celebrations were now breaking out, and the last faithful supporters of the patriotic anti-Nazi front prudently dispersed to make way for the crowd singing the *Horst-Wessel-Lied*.

From 12 March, planes had been landing at the airport in Vienna bringing the crack sections of the SS with Himmler at their head. Hitler himself was to arrive on 14 March, after a pilgrimage to his home town and a triumphal stop at Linz. The German army was expected on Sunday, 16 March, but did not arrive until the next day because of a bottleneck on the road from Linz to Vienna as the result of numerous breakdowns.[1]

With incredible enthusiasm, 90 per cent of the Austrian population voted by plebiscite for the *Anschluss*; as for the remaining 10 per cent, enemies real or supposed of the Nazi regime, many were arrested and locked up. In Germany a list of 1,742 names was published of people imprisoned. It was explained that the arrests had been carried out in order to place these individuals 'under protection from popular outbursts of feeling'. The Austrian army swore allegiance to the Führer on 14 March at 2000 hours: it had now ceased to exist, having been absorbed into the Wehrmacht according to the sacred plan: *Ein Volk, ein Reich, ein Führer*.

1 These breakdowns, caused by lack of fuel and the inexperience of some of the inadequately instructed troops, were interpreted by opponents of Germany as a demonstration of the weakness of the *Panzerdivisionen*. Their awakening was going to be brutal.

THE AUSTRIAN ARMY BEFORE THE ANSCHLUSS

1. Infantry, 4th regiment (Hoch und Deutschmeisterregiment) — 2. GHQ officer — 3. Transport troops corporal — 4. Dragoons lieutenant — 5. Generalmajor in service dress — 6. Dragoon of the 1st regiment

Ranks: 7. General — 8. Generalmajor — 9. Oberst — 10. Oberstleutnant — 11. Major — 12. Hauptmann, or Rittmeister, cavalry — 13. Oberleutnant — 14. Leutnant — 15. Vizeleutnant — 16. Offizierstellvertreter — 17. Stabswachtmeister — 18. Wachtmeister — 19. Zugführer — 20. Kaporal — 21. Gefreiter — 22. Soldat

Regimental facings (background for collar patches):
Grass green: infantry regiments 1, 2, and 3; alpine light infantry regiments 8 and 9; dragoons regiment 2; Tyrolean light infantry; train light infantry; alpine light infantry battalions 3 and 5

Sky blue: infantry regiment 4
Carmine: infantry regiment 5
Grey: infantry regiments 6 and 13
Sulphur yellow: infantry regiment 15
Black: infantry regiment 14 and train troops
Imperial yellow: 2nd squadron of 2nd dragoons regiment and 10th alpine light infantry regiment
Dark brown: infantry regiment 7
Orange: infantry regiment 12
Dark red: HQ and 2nd squadron of the 1st dragoons regiment
Black: GHQ
Scarlet: 3rd squadron and machine-gun squadron of 1st dragoons regiment, last battalion of the Guard and artillery
Blue-green: 11th infantry regiment, pioneers and radio
Light blue: baggage train and administration.
(taken from *Die Soldaten Europas*)

The German Army

THE BIRTH OF THE WEHRMACHT

As we have seen in the chapter on the Reichswehr, the army of a hundred thousand men born out of what the Germans henceforth unanimously called the 'Diktat of shame' was far from accepting the back-seat position which had been imposed on it by the Allies. It was, then, with considerable interest that the military leaders had taken up one of the points in a programme put forward by the leader of the new National Socialist Party. This programme openly and audaciously proclaimed its intention of replacing the Reichswehr with a proper national army. At last there existed in Germany a man who recognised the right of the army to exist, other than as a glorified police force suitable only for controlling terrorism.

The Munich 'putsch' and the events which subsequently threw Germany into a state of confusion, lasting right up to the day when the venerable Marshal Hindenburg named Hitler Chancellor of the Reich, further confirmed the Reichswehr in its confidence in the man who claimed the right to rearm his country. It was a startling attitude in the context of the Treaty of Versailles, yet it did not evoke any more positive reaction in the victors of 1918 than one of 'strong protest'; just as before every proposal, however well-intentioned, by political figures in Germany had been summarily dismissed. Soon, in the eyes of every German patriot, as poverty and unemployment disappeared, to be replaced by a decent standard of living and some remarkably effective social reforms, the National-Socialist dictatorship rapidly grew more palatable.

The events of 1934, brought on by the murder of Röhm[1] by the SA and the atrocities which attended the dissolution of the former traditional parties, brutally shattered the illusions of the idealists. But it was too late to resist. Those who tried were quickly made to see reason and were soon the first guests in the concentration camps set up for this purpose, while with an avalanche of admirably well worked-out

1 See p. 52.

68

propaganda, the Minister for Propaganda and Culture, Joseph Goebbels, was able to 'make the masses succumb to the power of words'.[2]

It is true to say, however, that the unity of the German people, supposedly manifested in mass demonstrations, was never as wholehearted as the Nazis might have hoped, or sometimes believed. The best proof of this, it would now seem, was the mere five million members[3] of the National Socialist Party in 1939, out of a population of more than seventy-five million.[4] But it is also true to say that whatever the size of the hold Hitler had on the German people, he would not have been able to drag his country into war by his own savage will alone.

One method implemented by Goebbels's propaganda machine seemed particularly efficient at firing the patriotic ardour of the German people —the use of coloured picture cards, presented in cigarette packets. Collected albums of these vignettes—depicting such things as the glorious history of Germany, loving descriptions of the armies of Frederick the Great, the War of Liberation from Napoleon, the dazzling victory over France in 1870—many of which were extremely beautiful, encouraged in every German a sense of past glories. Other albums, even more emotional, showed the

2 *Mein Kampf.*
3 The exact number is not known.
4 After the annexation of Austria.

GERMAN ARMY UNDER THE IIIrd REICH I

1–2. Ordinary or 2nd-class soldier 'Schütze'. (After October 1942 the ordinary soldier was called 'grenadier' according to the old tradition of Frederick the Great revived by Adolf Hitler; the title 'fusilier' was also attributed to certain units, usually as an honorary title). The Schütze here is standing to attention.

3–4. 1935 model helmet, left and right side. The shield in the national colours was gradually dropped during 1940. In 1943 the new model was to be stripped of all insignia — 5. Comparative sizes of 1935 and 1916 model helmets — 6. Belt buckle — 7. Pack with equipment for short marching exercises

8–27. Sidearm knots for the twenty companies comprising an infantry regiment of five battalions — 28. Special sword knot with its attaching cord in Russian calf, 3rd battalion of 67th infantry regiment, formerly 1st regiment of grenadiers in the Prussian Guard — 29. NCO's sidearm knot

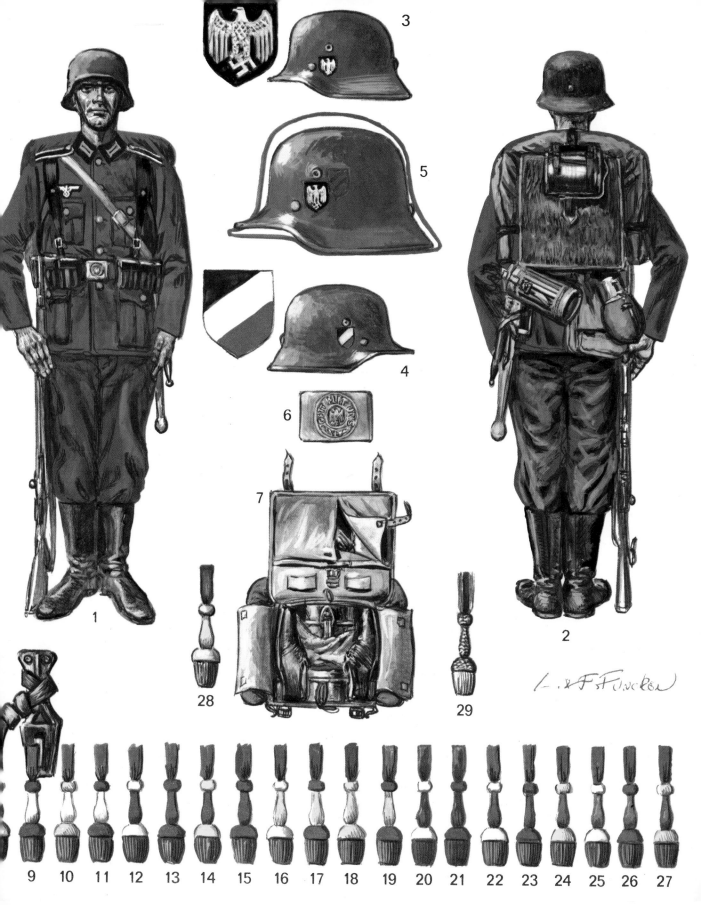

3

5

4

6

7

1

2

28

29

L & F Funcken

9 10 11 12 13 14 15 16 17 18 19 20 21 22 23 24 25 26 27

present poverty of the Reichswehr, now so vulnerable in the face of its enemies of yesterday, or depicted menacing neighbouring forces surrounding a crippled Germany. '*Wie die Anderen gerüstet sind... trotz vertraglicher Abrüstungspflicht*'—'How well everyone else is equipped... in spite of disarmament treaties'—such was the theme of one appeal, which, judging from the weapons shown, dates from about 1932.

Through these cards the authorities hoped not only to arouse patriotic emotions but also to instil a sense of fear into the German people. Pictures, as frightening as they were false, made propaganda out of the armed forces of dangerous neighbours by exaggerating their real strengths. One drawing shows a defenceless Germany in the grip of massed squadrons of the most advanced bombers, 8,900 strong as the caption informs the reader, of which three hundred were Belgian and seven hundred Czechoslovakian. (And yet in 1940 Belgium could muster only fourteen Fairey-Battle bombers!) The caption continues: '*In dieser Gefahr befinden wir uns!*'—'The danger in which we find ourselves!' Faced with such alarmism, the reactions of the German people could hardly be anything else but those of fear and anger. And it was these responses which led them to support whoever was able to give them back their pride and confidence.

Other forms of propaganda were used, showing equal skill in both captions and illustrations, to persuade the people of the excellence of National Socialism and the people's wisdom in choosing Hitler as their Führer. The strength of National Socialist youth was displayed on posters throughout the country, portraying stout healthy lads with resolute faces grouped around the new flag bearing the swastika: '*Und Ihr habt doch gesiegt*'—'And in spite of everything you have triumphed!' Later, an impressive poster was to symbolise Germany's first victories: the National Socialist flags flutter beneath the extended wings of an eagle ready to seize its next prey: '*Mit unsern Fahnen ist der Sieg!*'—'Victory goes with our flags!' The response of Germany's neighbours to these explosive slogans was paltry. There was for instance the famous French poster: 'We shall win because we are strongest', and a Belgian poster showed the minister responsible for the

fortresses in the east contemplating his work with complacency. However, in defence of these lacklustre propagandists it must be pointed out that they at least had no desire to lead their countrymen into another war.

GERMANY'S REARMAMENT

From the first days of the Hitler dictatorship the officer corps of the new Wehrmacht did its best to keep itself separate from the party; at the same time it adopted a conciliatory manner towards Hitler, an attitude dictated not only by the practicalities of the situation but also by their shared goal—Germany's greatness. But the army was soon to lose control of its own destiny, and to become no more than the play-thing of an all-powerful master.

One of Hitler's first moves was to renounce the Treaty of Versailles, which he did in 1935. He then immediately re-established conscription for all young Germans, who were compelled to do military service without exemption of any kind; the conscripts, who were called up at twenty, had already undergone military training in the ranks of one or other of the quasi-military organisations of the Reich and from about 1937 this highly efficient system would enable the Wehrmacht to mobilise a body of up to five million soldiers in forty-eight hours. Rearmament was now

GERMAN ARMY UNDER THE IIIrd REICH II

1. Stabsfeldwebel (infantry) in walking-out dress — 2. Artillery Oberfeldwebel in walking-out dress. On the sleeve is the insignia of 'Schirrmeister' or master saddler — 3. Feldwebel (mountain light infantry) in guard dress. On the chest is the lanyard of the marksman, as in fig. 1 — 4. Feldwebel attached to HQ, walking-out dress — 5. Unteroffizier of the chemical branch, battle dress — 6. Gefreiter in the artillery, walking-out dress — 7. Oberschütze or 1st-class soldier, later Obergrenadier (see preceding plate)

Arm insignia: 8. Gefreiter — 9. Obergefreiter — 10. Stabsgefreiter — 11. Obergefreiter (with more than 6 years' service)

12. National emblem — 13. Forage cap — 14. Cap, mountain light infantry — 15. Former Reichsheer uniform adapted to the new regulations — 16. Former Austrian army uniform adapted to the new regulations

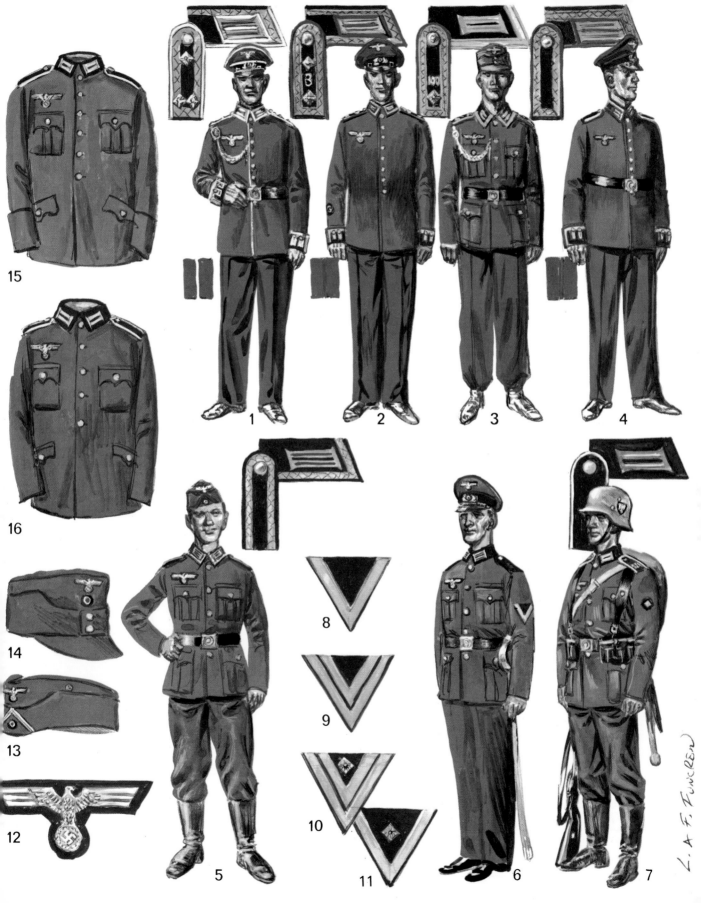

15

16

14

13

12

1

2

3

4

5

8

9

10

11

6

7

L. A F. Funcken

following a pattern of rapid and uninterrupted growth, thanks to the work which had already been discreetly undertaken by industrialists for several years. The Russians had opened up to the Germans her tank schools and aerodromes, and guns, aeroplanes and tanks had been studied and developed in secret. Retrospectively it seems a curious alliance, but it is explained by the old politics of Bismarck, who preached good relations with Russia; and in fact Russia herself, though Bolshevist since 1917, had been the first great power to negotiate on equal terms with Germany. Through this cooperation a sort of military camaraderie, which lasted from 1926 to at least 1930, had been established between the officers of the two nations.

THE NEW GERMAN SOLDIER

Superficially the new German infantryman hardly differed from the fighting man of 1918 or the soldier of the defunct Reichswehr, but a closer examination reveals several differences in the tunics. Some derived from the old army, others from the newly absorbed Austrian army, and the Wehrmacht preserved them for reasons of economy, contenting themselves with adding the symbol of the Third Reich, to be worn on the breast above the right pocket.

The helmet

Based on the 1916 model, which had been carefully studied by the surgeon August Bier and the craftsman armourer Franz Marx, the 1935 model was less ample in its proportions but, contrary to what is generally thought, almost as heavy: 1,300 grams as against 1,380. It was stamped from a single plate of sheet steel plated with chrome-nickel 1 mm thick. Painted matt grey, it bore on its right side the black, white and red national shield and on its left a black shield with a silver-grey eagle. These two badges, reproduced by means of decals, were on the majority of helmets in the German armed forces, but the air force and the Waffen-SS had special insignia. The 1935 steel helmet was obligatory for parades, guard duty, and in the field.

The Waffenrock

As in the old First World War army, initially all soldiers regardless of rank possessed at least two different uniforms. The first, which included the *Waffenrock*, was in some form Dress No. 1 and was worn on ceremonial occasions, for parade, and for going into town when off duty. The colour of the *Waffenrock* was called field grey, but this had changed since 1914 and it now had a light green tinge. The collar and cuffs were in dark blue-green badge cloth, decorated with braid and typically German stripes, called *Litzen*. The parade tunic, which was without front pockets, was fastened with eight white metal buttons. The national eagle, which was worn on the right breast, was of white metal lace for NCOs and soldiers, and in silver embroidery for officers. For generals gold replaced the silver.

The officer's *Waffenrock* served as his so-called 'society' uniform, report dress, service undress, and evening dress. For parade, officers wore the *Waffenrock* of the same cut but with a belt banded with silver and large plaited silver lanyards. Again, generals had the same in gold. After the outbreak of the war the *Waffenrock* was discontinued and gradually it disappeared.

GERMAN ARMY UNDER THE IIIrd REICH III

1. General, full arms, parade dress with cap — 2. Generaloberst, parade dress. (Colonel-in-chief of an artillery regiment). He is wearing the collar patches of that rank and arm of service with the shoulder straps of a Generaloberst — 3. Oberst, parade dress with helmet — 4. Oberst, battle dress with forage cap — 5. Oberstleutnant, parade dress — 6. Cavalry major in piped service tunic (undress) — 7. Hauptmann (artillery) battle dress — 8. Oberleutnant (mountain artillery) battle dress — 9. Leutnant of a Panzer Abteilung, parade dress with peaked cap

10. Peaked cap, general officer — 11. Old-style field cap for officers. This headgear became popular again particularly amongst the younger officers, who removed the stiffening from the crown of the peaked cap so that it looked more like the old-style field cap. Such bending of the regulations was especially common among tank troops and airmen — 12. Officer's new-style forage cap — 13. National emblem

14. Detail of the parade tunic collar, general officers (also worn by the ranks referred to in figs 14a–18). Shoulderstraps: 14a. Generalfeldmarschall — 15. General-oberst — 16. General, all arms — 17. Generalleutnant — 18. Generalmajor

The Feldbluse

The *Feldbluse* was the battle-dress tunic, much lighter in weight and more sombre than the *Waffenrock*. It had four gussetted pockets, and the distinctive braids and stripes of the regiment in more discreet form. All the silver parts, the *Litzen* and buttons, were matt grey. Fastened by only five buttons, the *Feldbluse* could be worn open during marching in summer, a practice which had already been authorised in the old Reichswehr and which was adopted by the Wehrmacht. (The precise ruling was that only the first and second buttons could be undone.) In certain cases the *Feldbluse* was used as evening dress, when the two back belt hooks were replaced by two uniform buttons.

The officer's battle dress was similar to that of the other ranks, with the badges equally unobtrusive, except for generals. This uniform also served as undress and walking-out dress. Another uniform, reserved for officers, was the *Feldbluse mit Vorstossen*. It was similar to the *Feldbluse* but had additional piping, as the German name indicates. The piping ran the length of the fastening of the tunic as well as around the collar and cuffs. This uniform was most often used as service undress, when it was worn without a belt.

A white tunic, also exclusive to officers, was the *Weisser Rock*, which could be worn in barracks and in training camps but was not used out of doors except on horseback. Fastened with eight buttons, and with four patch pockets, it had no ornaments except shoulder straps and the traditional emblem on the breast. The collar was completely white.

Trousers

Trousers were iron grey for all ranks, except for the air force, which had a uniform of a special colour, and the armoured troops. Officers alone could wear riding breeches, which were trimmed with a braid the colour of their arms. General officers were allowed a very wide scarlet stripe divided by two fine iron grey lines, with the officers of GHQ having the same stripe but in carmine. Specially designed trousers were created for the regiments of the *Gebirgsjäger*—the mountain infantry. Following the style of ski trousers, they were tight at the ankle and could only be worn with laced boots.

GERMAN ARMY UNDER THE IIIrd REICH IV

Hats, collars and shoulder straps: 1. Generalarzt (doctor) — 2. Stabsarzt (doctor) — 3. Unterapotheker (pharmacist) — 4. Sanitätsunteroffizier — 5. Unterveterinär — 6. Major, music inspector — 7. Oberleutnant, director of music — 8. Generalleutnant, Ministry inspector — 9. Generalmajor of the Reich Council of War — 10. Oberstleutnant of the Reich Council of War — 11. Oberst of the Court Martial — 12. Councillor Major at army Supreme GHQ — 13. Feld Bischof, Roman Catholic (Field Bishop) — 14. Senior chaplain (Protestant)

Special insignia: 15. Flag bearer (right arm) — 16. Smoke-screen bomb thrower (left forearm). Insignia of specialist soldiers (right forearm) — 17. Medical personnel — 18. Farrier — 19. Armourer — 20. Artificier — 21. Saddler — 22. Radio — 23. Master saddler — 24. Feldwebel of fortified works — 25. Feldwebel engineer for fortifications — 26. Carrier-pigeon handler — 27. Artillery gun-layer special insignia (left forearm)

Advance infantry standard signals: 28. 'We are here!' — 29. 'Territory clear of enemy!' — 30. 'Territory occupied by enemy!' — 31. 'We are digging in!', or 'Dig in!' — 32. 'Munitions to the fore!' — 33. 'Danger, gas!'

2

3

4

5

6

7

8

9

13

14

15

16

17

18

19

20

21

22

23

24

25

26

27

28

29

30

31

32

33

Headgear

The Feldmütze: This was the headgear of the troops in battle. It was a side cap, field grey like the tunic, and had as its insignia the national emblem, a cockade in the German colours, and an inverted chevron in the arm of service colour. This type of cap was adopted by officers after 6 June 1938, but with the addition of silver piping on the scallop at the front and along the upper seam of the cap. This style was worn up to the rank of colonel; generals' field caps were piped in gold.

The Bergmütze: This type of headgear, known by civilians as a *Skimütze,* was the mountain infantry's headgear. It had a cloth peak and the usually turned-up brim could be turned down to cover the neck and ears in cold weather. This cap was later (1943) made a general issue item throughout the army and was then called *Einheitmütze.*

The Schirmmütze:[1] Literally peaked cap. This was the standard pattern for all soldiers, NCOs and officers, and had as its main characteristic a false chin strap, in black leather for soldiers and NCOs up to the rank of sergeant-major, in silver up to the rank of colonel, and in gold for generals. Soldiers and NCOs were not allowed to wear this cap in the field.

The overcoat

The overcoat was field grey in colour and was of the same cut for all ranks, though the quality of the material was better for officers. The turned-down collar was of a dark blue-green material. The overcoat had to be completely buttoned up. Only generals could wear it half open and the revers thus exposed had scarlet facings. Generals were also the only rank with gilt buttons.

1 This was not an 'issue' item: officers, of course, bought all their own clothing, while other ranks had to buy this particular item if they wanted one.

RANK

The different German army ranks are shown in the table overleaf with their approximate equivalents in the British and French armies. All these ranks were distinguished by special insignia on the left arm only, or on the collar and shoulder tabs. Specialist insignia were worn mainly on the right forearm.[2]

2 Details of ranks and the main insignia are given in the illustrations.

GERMAN ARMY, ARMS AND EQUIPMENT I

1–6. Light assault equipment

Pistols: 7. 9 mm Luger 08 — 8. 9 mm Walther P 38 — 9. 7·63 mm Mauser, 1912 model — 10. 7·65 mm Mauser HSc — 11. 7·65 mm Sauer model 38 — 12. 7·65 mm Walther PPK

Rifle, carbines and sub-machine guns: 13. 98 model rifle — 14. 98 model carbines — 15. 98 K (Kurz-short) model carbine. These three weapons were all of 7·92 mm calibre. The 98 K carbine was the most widely distributed of the three — 16. MP 18 (Maschinenpistole) Bergmann (9 mm) — 17. 9 mm MP 34 Bergmann — 18. 9 mm MP 35 Bergmann specially made for the Waffen-SS. These three weapons had horizontal loading belts — 19. 9 mm MP 38 Beretta — 20. 9 mm MP 38 Erma, wrongly attributed to Schmeisser, who did no more than perfect it under the name MP 40 — 21.9 mm MP 40 Schmeisser. More than a million of these weapons were produced, and it was by far the most celebrated of the light arms of the last war. Some units, such as parachute troops, used an MP 40 with modified magazine taking a double charge of 2×32 bullets.

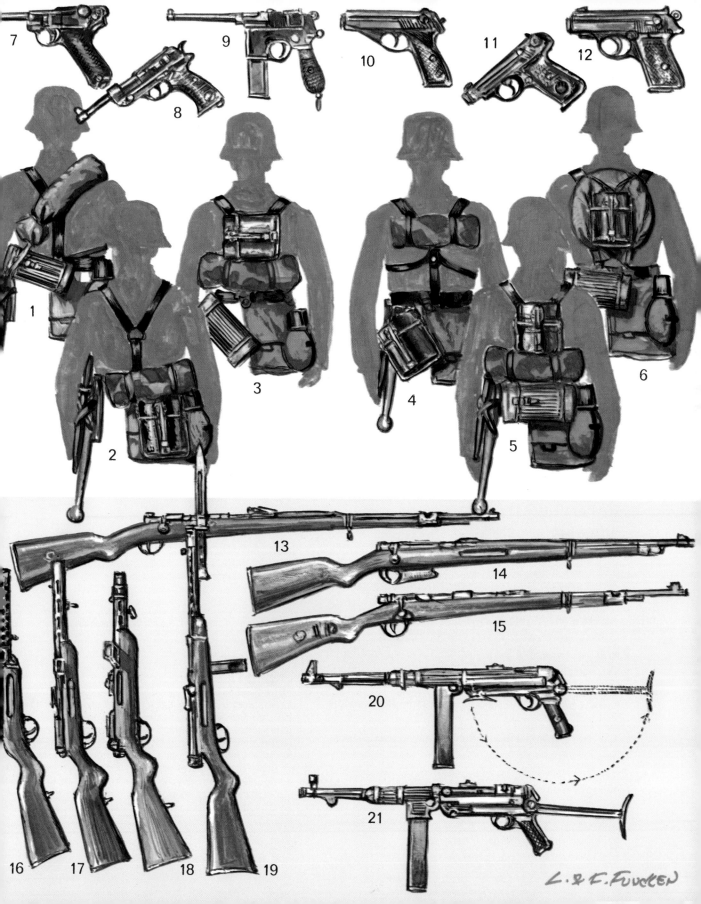

Schütze	Private	Soldat de deuxième classe
Oberschütze	Private (senior)	(Soldat confirmé)
Gefreite	Lance-corporal	Soldat de première classe
Obergefreite	Corporal	(Exempt supérieur)
Unteroffizier	Lance-sergeant	Caporal et caporal-chef
Unterfeldwebel	Sergeant	Sergent ou maréchal des logis
Feldwebel	Company sergeant-major	Sergent-chef ou maréchal des logis-chef.
Oberfelwebel	Sergeant-major	Adjudant
Hauptfeldwebel	Regimental sergeant-major	—
Stabsfeldwebel	Staff sergeant	Adjudant-chef
Leutnant	Second lieutenant	Sous-lieutenant
Oberleutnant	Lieutenant	Lieutenant
Hauptmann	Captain	Capitaine
Major	Major	Chef de bataillon ou d'escadron (commandant)
Oberstleutnant	Lieutenant-colonel	Lieutenant-colonel
Oberst	Colonel	Colonel
—	Brigadier	—
	Major-general	
Generalmajor	Lieutenant-general	Général de brigade
Generalleutnant	General	Général de division
General der Infanterie, Kavallerie, Artillerie...	General	Général de corps d'armée
Generaloberst	Field Marshal	Général d'armée
Generalfeldmarschall	—	Maréchal

SIDEARM KNOTS

The knot hanging from the end of the bayonet or sabre, called a *Troddel* in the infantry and a *Faustriemen* in the cavalry, made it possible to identify precisely which unit its bearer belonged to. The arms colour, which was anyway found only in the piping, was not allowed to show such details as the number of the battalion and company. But through its different component parts (the strap, the slide, the stem, the crown and the tassels) and through an ingenious arrangement of its six colours, the knot gave all the necessary information—though one needed a great deal of experience to be able to read such an identity card! The whole business, moreover, was further complicated by the special knots carried by NCOs, which bore no relation to the company colours. Officers were issued with a special model, which was silver-coloured, called a *Portepée*.

GERMAN ARMY, ARMS AND EQUIPMENT II

1. 7·92 mm MG 15 (Maschinengewehr). Although designed for the air force this weapon was modified for ground combat — 2. 7·92 mm MG 13 Dreyse. This relic of the 1914-1918 war was the forerunner of the celebrated MG 34 — 3. 7·92 mm MG 34 mounted on its tripod — 4. MG 34 on bipod. The MG 34 was the first purpose machine gun available in two forms, light and middle-weight. Ironically, it was devised by German engineers to conform with the restrictions of the Treaty of Versailles, which forbade Germany to possess heavy machine guns. One man could operate the light version provided that he used the drum magazine holding 50 cartridges, or the double drum magazine with 75 cartridges. Figure 4 shows a marksman ready to fire with the flexible 50-cartridge band, which required the use of a sight. The heavier version, on a tripod, needed a team of three men and used flexible belts of 50 cartridges, which could be joined end to end, thus ensuring particularly fierce continuous fire. When used for continuous fire, the overheated barrel could be dismantled and replaced by another in a few seconds.

Anti-tank guns: 5. Panzerbüchse Px 38 (7·92 mm) — 6. Panzerbüchse S 18 Solothurn (20 mm) — 7–8. Hand grenades

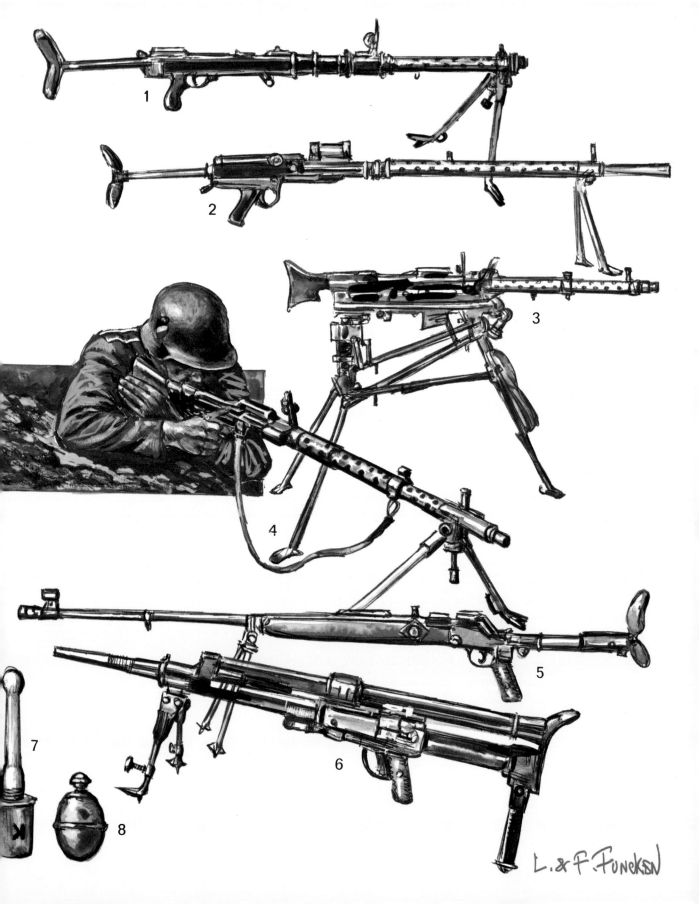

PERSONAL WEAPONS FROM 1939 TO 1941

Guns

The 'standard issue' weapons to infantrymen were the rifle and the carbine Mauser 1898 model, 7·92 mm, weighing respectively 4 kg and 3·2 kg. The bayonet, which had come into service in 1900, had a 250 mm blade, and was the basic model from which many variations were developed. A standard bayonet measuring 312 mm was developed specifically for the Wehrmacht in 1933. It was adapted for the 33/40 rifle which was issued to mountain infantry and parachutists.

Pistols

Well known everywhere, the 9 mm Luger Parabellum was still very much in favour but it had a serious rival, which was adopted in 1938, the Walther P38, a Parabellum of the same calibre.

Machine pistols

Several models of this type of weapon, such as the *Maschinenpistole* MP18 Bergmann, the MP28 Schmeisser, the MP34 Erma and the MP38 Beretta, had been used in the paramilitary Nazi movements and later in the army, but the most celebrated German automatics were the famous MP38 Erma and MP40 Schmeisser, which largely replaced the models with wooden butts.

Machine guns

The *Maschinengewehr* model 34 was used as either a light or a heavier machine gun depending on whether the bipod or the tripod was used with it. It could fire cylindrical magazines or belts of fifty cartridges which were connected to each other by an ingenious system to ensure continuous fire. Other less well known types were used in the early campaigns, such as the Czech ZB26, the Dreyse MG13, the Madsen MG37, and the Solothurn 38. All these machine guns used the standard 7·92 cartridges.

SOVIET ARMY 1938 TO JANUARY 1943 I

Insignia and ranks, collar patches and forearm stripes:
1. Marshal — 2. Army general — 3. General colonel —
4. Lieutenant general — 5. Major general

Insignia from the shirt collar, the turned-down collar of the tunic or overcoat and the stripes carried on the forearm:
6. Colonel. Enlarged detail of commanding officers' insignia
— 7. Lieutenant-colonel — 8. Major — 9. Captain —
10. First lieutenant. Detail of the insignia — 11. Lieutenant
— 12. Sub-lieutenant

NB: All these ranks are shown in the colours of the infantry except for that of the marshal, which is scarlet, a colour reserved for officers of HQ. The general officers could wear the straight collar decorated with the parallelograms shown in figs 6-12, but with the ruby lozenge and a gold star. The army general wore four lozenges and one star; the general colonel, three lozenges and one star, etc. This practice had fallen into disuse on the eve of the war, and only high rank at the Commissariat of the People, as well as more conservative officers, still wore them.

13. General officer in tunic — 14. General officer in overcoat — 15. Commanding officer in shirt

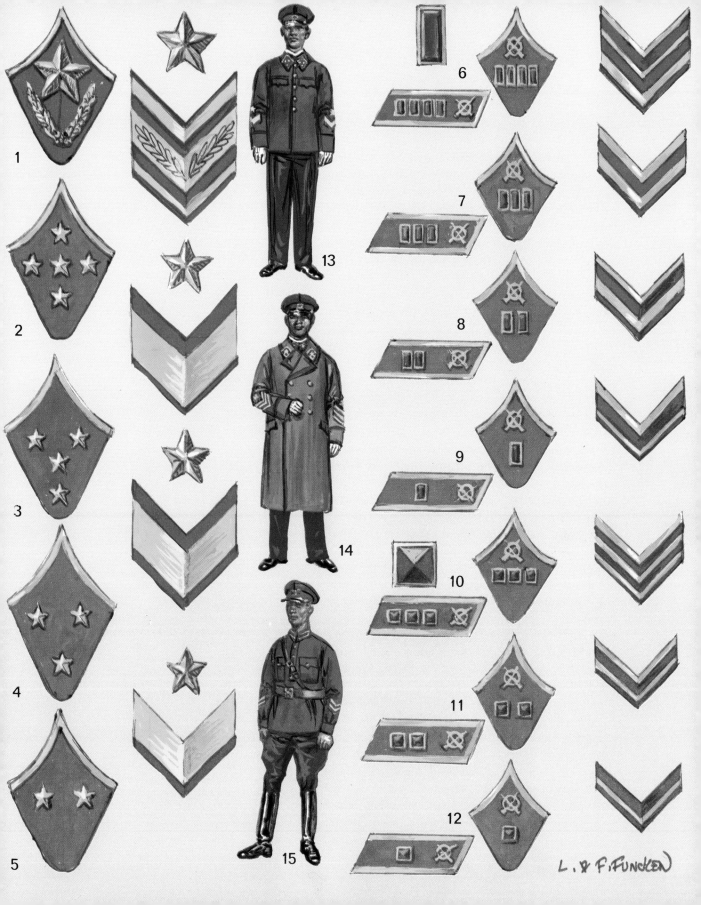

The Russian Army from 1918 to 1941

In 1917 the Tsar's army was replaced by the new revolutionary army, a force which was at least 50 per cent Bolshevik. The military organisation of the revolutionaries had also created powerful 'worker guards' in the main industrial centres, and it was from these units that the Red Guard was created when, on 8 November 1917, the Second Soviet Congress founded the first People's government and also the 'People's Commissariat for the Army' which was required to form a regular Red army. This Red army—its full title was the Workers' and Peasants' Red Army—was finally created after the Third Congress of January 1918. It was based on voluntary enlistment.

Right from the beginning the young army had to withstand a concerted attack from several fronts simultaneously: from the 'Whites' who wanted to restore the old regime; from the Allied contingent; and even from certain outspoken German bodies. Commanded by both the Commissars of the People and those Tsarist officers who had gone over to the new regime, the new army had to lie very low in order to survive these threats.

However, in spite of the commissars' excessive powers, and their instinctive distrust of the ex-Tsarist officers, born leaders like Tukhachevski and Budënny, as well as the out-and-out militants like Voroshilov and Timoshenko, managed to organise things very successfully. The volunteer system had quickly been replaced by conscription, but only peasants and workers had the honour of defending their country under arms. A powerful cavalry was created, raised to repulse the White troops led by Denikin which were threatening Moscow; to the war cry 'People to Horseback' the first Red cavalry to be mounted dispersed the Whites. Then 1920 saw the rapid disbandment of the Allied contingents, who were sickened with suffering and dying for a cause about which they hardly cared. Nevertheless it took another two years before the country was finally rid of the last remnants of the White army in Karelia, Siberia and the Ukraine, and even in the government in Moscow.

THE ARMY AND THE MILITIA

It now became necessary to organise the demobilisation of an army which by January 1921 had grown from a hundred thousand men in 1918 to four million. The army was completely reorganised, and in 1924 reduced to a permanent force of 562,000 men. Eighty-five per cent of the officers in this new regular army had taken an active part in the battles of the Civil War, and 48 per cent of these belonged to the Communist Party.

Peripheral to the regular army were the territorial militia, in which all citizens were enlisted. After an initial period of military training which was completed at their place of work, from the age of twenty-one young Soviet men were sent off to a military training camp for three or four months' training periods which were repeated over five consecutive years. Throughout these periods of training the militiaman received two-thirds of his civilian salary, his job was guaranteed, and he enjoyed full national insurance benefits. Up to the age of twenty-four the militiaman was part of the first call-up, at which age he passed into the second call-up group until he was forty. Citizens considered unworthy to bear arms, that is those who were not workers or peasants or employees in one of the state institutions, had to serve in various work forces, but only in time of war. Since, however, these 'suspect

SOVIET ARMY 1938 TO JANUARY 1943 II

1. Chief adjutant — 2. Adjutant with detail of the infantry insignia — 3. Staff sergeant of cavalry — 4. Sergeant in the engineers — 5. Corporal of the chemical branch — 6. First entirely Soviet-style helmet worn by *élite* troops from 1936 until the end of 1941 — 7. Helmet introduced in 1941 and worn throughout the army — 8. Budionovka, the oldest Soviet military headgear worn from 1917 to at least 1941

9. Infantry, summer dress — 10. Infantry, winter dress — 11. Cavalryman, winter dress — 12. Pioneer, summer dress. Apart from the insignia it was the same dress as worn in 1914 — 13. Infantryman in full winter dress

NB: In the course of 1942 the insignia worn by the infantry on their collars (target and crossed rifles) was dropped and worn only by the troops of the NKVD.

1

2

3

4

5

6

7

8

9

10

11

12

13

L. x F. Funcken

persons' did no active military service, they were obliged to pay a compensatory military tax, amounting to between 50 and 100 per cent on their taxable income up to the age of twenty-five, subsequently dropping to 25 per cent by the age of forty.

The Red army proper enlisted only 270,000 conscripts out of the eight hundred to nine hundred thousand available men each year.

POLITICAL EDUCATION

A special political section looked after the political education of the soldier, a part of training which was thought to be most important and which occupied a large part of the time spent on improving the general cultural level of the proletarian conscript. No unit, however small, was without its political instructor, who was on an equal footing with any other officer in the unit when it came to political and cultural matters. The ultimate aim of the political section, as well as making the Red soldier aware of his role as defender of the workers' state, was to turn him into an active collaborator in socialist enlightenment once he returned to civilian life.

THE SUMMER CAMP[1]

The Red army summer camp was situated near Moscow, on the road from Leningrad. Summer manoeuvres were alternated with a wide variety of entertainments which included the theatre, cinema, music and chess. The soldiers lived in spacious tents, in groups of eight along with their section chief.

THE MARCHING COMPETITION

This event—ten kilometres to be covered, in full battle dress—was a military exercise which had the added attraction of being a competition. After a medical examination by the regimental doctor each company, ranked in four columns, set off at 1130 hours in the

1 Curiously, the summer camp owes its name to the October Revolution of 1917.

hot sun, marching behind their platoon leader. The record time to beat was 1 hour 45 minutes.

The first kilometre was easy, and often it was necessary to hold back the more exuberant soldiers. Come the second kilometre, however, and the order was given to put on gas masks, which after about a hundred metres soon became most uncomfortable, but for those who tried to remove the stifling masks an officer was on the look-out. By the end of this second kilometre the men were on the verge of exhaustion, their bodies bathed in sweat. The ragged columns were now reorganised under the officer's order to 'form ranks', and hastily removing their masks the men covered the next two kilometres at a rapid march. Next, after traversing a precipitous ravine and crossing a railway line, the men arrived at an immense firing range. Here, deployed in extended order, the companies had to crawl two hundred metres, then at the command 'stand up' fire five cartridges in one minute at targets appearing every ten seconds. Every two minutes the leader of each platoon informed his men of the time they were making, and the urgent pace intensified as the soldiers came first to a steep descent and then a rough climb. At this point hand grenades, which the soldiers were carrying in their haversacks, were thrown and the race continued. Now there was a bayonet charge at a forest of stakes piled around with sandbags, and then a river which had to be crossed with the aid of thin tree trunks. Once on the other side a barbed wire entanglement had to be negotiated.

SOVIET ARMY 1938 TO JANUARY 1943 III

1–3. Soldier and officers of the NKVD — 4. Terek Cossack wearing kubanka on his head — 5. Cossack from the Don, with kubanka

Hat badges worn on the forage cap and on the budionovka — 6. Infantry — 7. Cavalry — 8. Engineers — 9. Forage cap known as pilotka — 10. Cavalryman's budionovka — 11. Uchanka, which was to replace the old pointed cap throughout the army

Distinguishing insignia: 12. NKVD — 13. Infantry — 14. Cavalry — 15. Engineers — 16. Kuban and Terek Cossacks — 17. Don Cossacks — 18. General officer's cap insignia — 19. Insignia for cap, uchanka, and forage cap; for the latter, from 1941 onwards. The arm of service colour around the turn up and upper seam, and behind the star, was dropped after the first campaigns in Finland.

2

13

4

15

6

17

18

19

1

2

3

6

7

8

9

10

11

4

5

L. & F. Funcken

The road they now reached was extremely dusty, and it was often too at this stage that the stronger men had to carry the rifles of their weaker comrades. At last the camp was reached, and with a final surge of energy they charged. The record which had seemed so easy to beat was rarely equalled. After another medical examination there were further physical exercises to complete before the exhausted soldiers were allowed to relax. Then the next day the winners' prize was presented by the commanding officer—a gleaming accordion.

MANOEUVRES

In these early days of the Red army there was usually a five-day period of manoeuvres which took place during the rainy season and in which the entire regiment participated. On the first day the soldiers would set off on a night march, and during the short rest periods which they were from time to time allowed the accordion was taken out of its case and the best dancers in the regiment would perform for their comrades. Hardened by life in the summer camp, the Ukrainian and Russian dancers proved that they were able to continue their musical and dance interludes throughout the five days without losing their lightness and agility.

The most dreaded enemy was the mud, that famous Russian mire which the Wehrmacht was to get to know in the not too distant future. It is interesting to note here that the strategic and tactical importance of this mud was well known to the officers, one of whom remarked as early as 1928 that 'every invading army would be brought to a halt by it'. Another important aspect of these manoeuvres was the establishment of regimental quarters in villages, through which the soldiers and peasants, talking together around the communal samovar, learned to live with one another. There were further manoeuvres, using artillery and machine guns, until at last when the exercise was over the regiments returned to their barracks and the militiamen to their factories or fields; for these militiamen the 'reservist service' had lasted for six weeks.

THE BARRACKS

After the fall of the Tsarist regime the barracks, which had been allowed to fall into some disrepair, were restored to habitability. Every October walls were whitewashed, mattresses shaken up and bedclothes aired in preparation for the new conscripts. Red streamers welcomed these new recruits when they arrived, encouraging them to learn the skills of war in the Red Army School in order that they may be better able to defend the worker state.

The young soldier was first provided with his uniform, and his head was shaved. He then had to learn how to address his superiors in the correct way, 'comrade officer', and also not to use this title outside the army. At the first assembly the 'political committee' for each company was elected, and the next day the first 'wall diary' appeared, through which the company would learn to express its impressions, observations and criticisms.

The wall diary, an idea conceived and developed during the Civil War, had become one of the most important outward signs of political life in the Soviet Union. Obviously it assumed greater or lesser importance according to particular circumstances, but it was in use everywhere—in factories and young communist clubs as well as in the barracks. Its purpose was to improve the cultural level and above all the

SOVIET ARMY 1938 TO JANUARY 1943 IV

1. 1891/30 rifle — 2. 1891/30 with sight for master marksman. Enlarged view of sight, left side

3. Anti-tank gunner with his ammunition server holding a Simonov anti-rank rifle

4. Degtiarev anti-tank rifle. There were a great many of these clumsy lead contraptions in use in the Soviet regiments. They were virtually powerless against medium-weight armour plate, although in the hands of determined soldiers they could be surprisingly effective — 5. Tokarev TT 7·62 mm pistol — 6. Sub-machine gun M34/38 (7·62 mm) — 7. PPD model sub-machine gun, 1940 (7·62 mm) — 8. 1938 carbine (7·62 mm) — 9. Hand grenades — 10. Degtiarev DP automatic rifle, 7·62 mm (the bipod is hidden by the machine gun below it) — 11. Heavy machine gun, Maxim 1910 model

political awareness of the masses, to foster closer contact between officers and soldiers, and to develop the practice of self-criticism, which it was hoped would eliminate faults, negligence and mistakes, at whatever level they might occur.

MILITARY SERVICE

The recruit arrived at the barracks in October and his training continued until May. During the initial period of his training the conscripts were known as 'young Red soldiers', a name they would keep until they had sworn allegiance to the red flag. Reveille was at 0630 hours, when the recruits assembled in the barracks square, without overcoat or belt, their hands wrapped in felt to protect them against the often Arctic temperatures of 20° or more below freezing.

(hours) 0700 After fifteen minutes of physical training the recruit went back to his sleeping quarters, put on his overcoat, and had a breakfast of thick soup.

0730 Roll call, kit and clothes inspection (rifles were inspected twice weekly).

0800 Practical and theoretical training in the square or classroom.

1000 Political and general education classes.

1100 Tactical instruction, group firing practice, bayonet fighting.

1200 The study of army regulations relating to guard duty and general discipline, and the theory of gun handling.

1400 Private study, with commentaries, questions and explanations of any points not understood.

1500 Dinner: a thick soup with meat, one additional dish, bread and tea.

1530-1700 Compulsory rest. This period was known as the 'dead hour'.

1700-2300 Relaxation, during which the men could go into the local town, to a club, or to the sports room for table tennis or other sports. The wall diary was filled in during this period. Then roll call and lights out.

THE WINTER MARCH

The snow, which covered vast areas of the land for long periods, made marching in formation very difficult, and once a week the various regiments had to carry out a trip on skis. Roused at 0330 hours, the soldiers swallowed their soup and hot tea and assembled in the square. If the thermometer registered more than 30° below zero the exercise was postponed, if not the infantrymen put on their skis and long white-hooded robes (known as 'snow shirts') and set off, section by section, into the night.

THE GROWTH OF THE ARMY

The widespread rearmament throughout Europe incited Russia also to increase her army, which developed rapidly from two million men in 1937 to over four million by 1941. Rank had by this date been re-established, albeit very cautiously, and a second important stage in this development was to occur in January 1943.[1]

1 The new insignia of rank in the Red army will be described in vol. 4.

CZECHOSLOVAKIAN ARMY I

Rank insignia: 1. General — 2. Colonel — 3. Lieutenant-colonel — 4. Major — 5. Captain-commandant — 6. Captain — 7. Lieutenant — 8. Second lieutenant — 9. Adjudant — 10. Sergeant-major — 11. Section chief — 12. Corporal — 13. Private — 14. Lance-corporal — 15. Gendarmerie cap badge

Arms colours: 16. Infantry — 17. Artillery — 18. Air force — 19. Cavalry — 20. Engineers — 21. Signals — 22. Motorised troops maintenance — 23. Artillery maintenance — 24. Air force maintenance

25. Forage cap — 26. New-style helmet, 1934

27. Superior officer in battle dress — 28. Infantryman with old-style helmet — 29. Infantry officer in battle dress

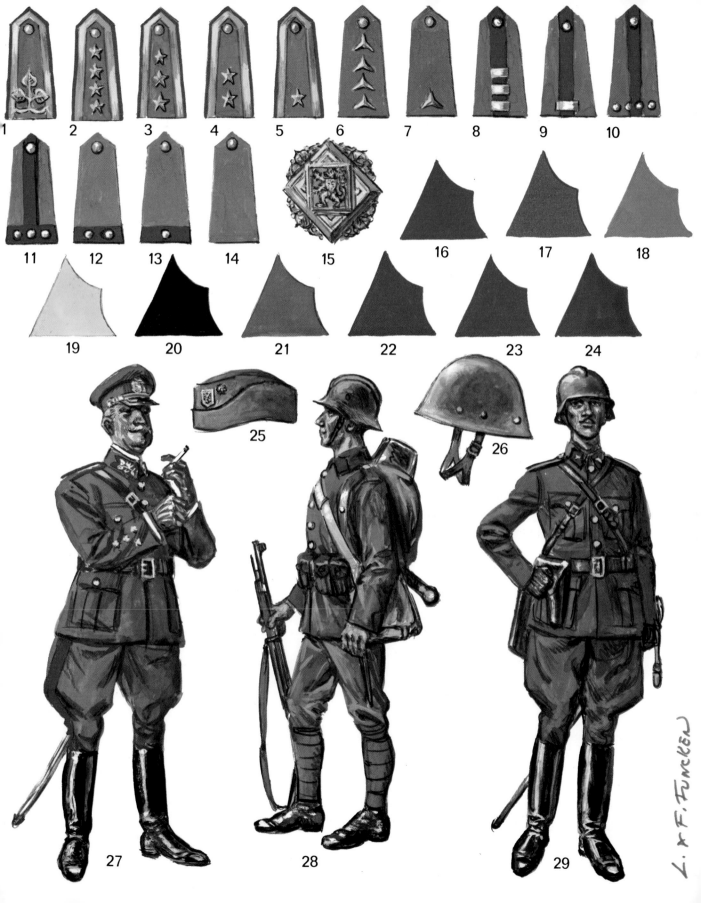

Czechoslovakia

Created from bits and pieces wrested from the losers of the First World War, Czechoslovakia was a real hotch-potch of peoples, among whom the Czechs and the Slovaks were the most numerous.

The newly formed country was soon to feel the consequences of its racial difficulties, which anyway many of its people had already experienced under Austro-Hungarian rule. After 1919, bloody incidents broke out between the authorities and the Germanic minority groups in Moravia. Other minorities were also to cause problems for the government—the Hungarians, the Poles, the Ukrainians in Ruthenia, and above all the Germans who had inherited the German-Czech border lands, the famous Sudetens. On top of all this there were distinct feelings of animosity between the agricultural and Catholic Slovaks and the anti-religious Czechs.

The advent of Nazism sent hopes soaring among the Germans in Sudetenland, Moravia and Bohemia, who immediately formed two groups whose obvious goal was unity with the great German nation. In 1932 the Czech government attempted to resist this movement by condemning certain Bohemian Nazis of the *Volksport* for conspiracy against the republic. Then in 1933 the Sudeten Nazi Party, which from 1929 had had eight deputies in the Czech Parliament, was dissolved.

German-Czech relations further deteriorated when the government in Prague began to apply discriminatory measures against the Sudeten Germans, who (unfortunately for the Czechs) occupied the fortified frontier zone. In addition, employment in the heavy industry of these areas began to get suspiciously scarce for people of German origin. The whole situation, admittedly difficult enough already, was freely exploited by propagandists of Nazi persuasion, who even managed to attract the Catholic Sudetens, who until then had been anti-Hitler.

In October 1933 Konrad Henlein founded the *Sudetendeutsche Heimatfront*—the patriotic Sudeten German Front—which re-formed the various associations that had been dissolved. Then in 1935 this party, now more modestly rechristened the Sudeten Party, demanded from the Czech government the creation of a federal state and a foreign policy based on unity with Germany. Faithful to her allies, and still retaining confidence in the power of the League of Nations, the Czech government quietly strengthened its fortifications along the German frontier and turned a deaf ear to these demands. In fairness to the Sudetens, however, it must be conceded that from this time on some Czech administrators and the police began to ingore or flout the Sudetens' proper rights as Czech citizens. President Beneš himself was angered by these injustices, and genuinely tried to get the rights of all the minority groups properly respected. Unity was achieved between the Slovaks and the anti-Nazi Sudetens, but Henlein and his followers systematically refused all approaches, seeking only to aggravate the situation. Worse, in 1938 the Sudeten Party leader proclaimed his right to adopt and teach the ideals of Hitler's National Socialism. The annexation of Austria by Hitler in 1938 strengthened the position of the minority groups hostile to the Czech president, and in the face of this new menace he ordered the partial mobilisation of Czech troops. A first attempt at British mediation failed. Then Neville Chamberlain, the British prime minister, brought together with him in conference the French President Daladier and George Bonnet (the French foreign minister); after long deliberation they communicated their proposals to the Czech government, inviting the Czechs to agree to the dismemberment of their country.

In his broadcast to the Czech people the president said, 'We stand alone. We are sacrificing ourselves for

CZECHOSLOVAKIAN ARMY II

1. Infantryman in the field with new-style helmet (this was rarely worn) — 2. Gendarme — 3. National Guard — 4. Flying officer — 5. National cockade, air force — 6. Breast insignia, airman — 7. Tail insignia — 8. Emblem painted on aircraft fuselage — 9. Letov — 10. Avia 8-534

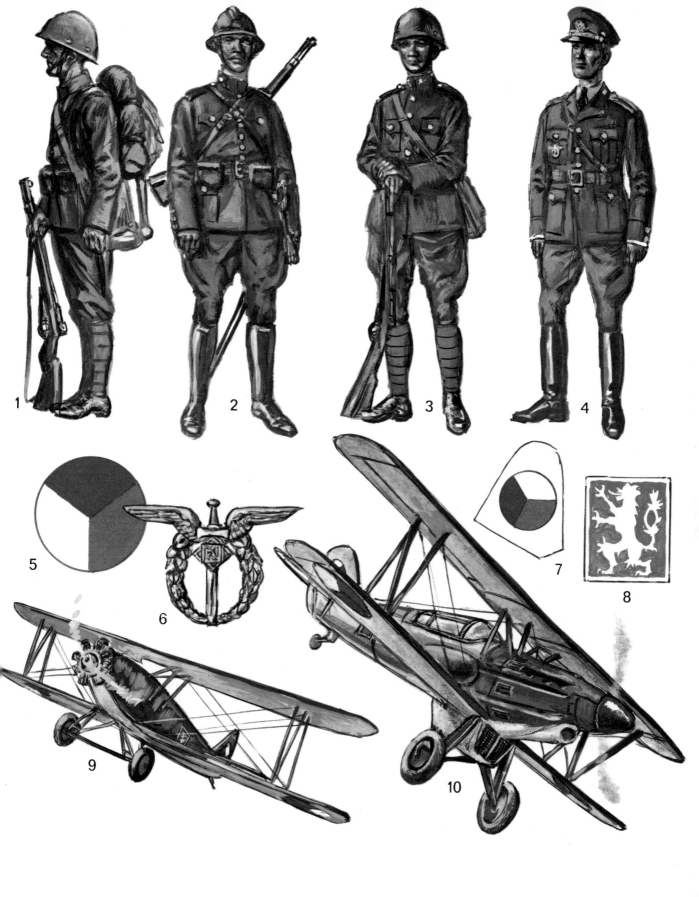

the safety of Europe.' It was an agonising sacrifice, which, as future events were soon to reveal, was all in vain. The carving up of Czechoslovakia, fixed by the Munich Agreement of 30 September 1938, which was signed by Chamberlain, Daladier, Mussolini and Hitler, involved all those areas whose populations were more than 50 per cent of German extraction. The Czechs raised several objections: what would happen to their fortifications, which were mainly in Sudetenland? And their heavy industry, which was in the same area, was that too to be handed over to the Reich? But who could argue with Hitler, now that he had become the law-maker of Europe? In Prague the population came out in protest, demanding that the frontiers be defended. They were not. On 5 October President Beneš resigned and left the country, and on 10 October the dismemberment began. Nor were the Germans the only ones to rush in for the spoils; Hungary and Poland both snatched several pieces from the stricken republic, a fact which is often overlooked.

In the whole operation Czechoslovakia lost one-third of her population: three and a half million to the Reich, nearly a million to Hungary, and more than 230,000 to Poland. Among the annexed people there were over a million Czechs and Slovaks who inevitably lost those rights which up to this time had been guaranteed to the ethnic minorities in Czechoslovakia. The final break-up was now not long in coming. Convinced of its powerlessness, and completely abandoned by its former allies, on 14 March 1939 the Czech government 'put the destiny of her people in the hands of the Führer'. The 140,000 men of the Czechoslovakian army, who had been forced to stand by helplessly throughout, were deprived of their arms and disbanded. There was rage in their hearts but there was nothing they could do, though a handful of pilots did manage to escape by the only route left open, the air. One such, Josef František, was even daring enough to launch a single-handed attack on the German columns with his old-fashioned fighter plane. Taking refuge in Poland, he was to fight with his Polish comrades in arms against the German invader, and after their defeat to go on to join the ranks of the RAF, where he was to be one of their finest pilots in the Battle of Britain.

The Polish Army

Czechoslovakia had no sooner been engulfed than another threatening cloud began to darken the skies of the still resolutely optimistic pacifists. This time it was to Poland that Hitler turned, in his compassionate concern for the 'oppressed German minority groups' there. What was the Führer claiming this time? First, he wanted the annexation of the free town of Danzig; second, the right to construct a motorway to connect eastern Prussia to the rest of the Reich, using foreign territory across the Polish 'corridor'. It was a foregone conclusion that Poland, secure in the support of France and Britain, would not agree. In Paris President Daladier, his Munich illusions finally shattered, declared in a radio broadcast: 'Why, today, does the Danzig question run the risk of unleashing war across Europe? It is because, proposed as it has been with threats of force, and bringing in its wake far greater territorial demands, it raises the whole question of the existence and freedom of Poland... It is the future of the peoples of Europe which is actually in question. It is our destiny, too, people of France.'

POLISH ARMY I

1–3. Infantrymen — 4. Subaltern officer — 5. General — 6. Cavalryman — 7. Cavalryman in overcoat — 8. Airman — 9. Sailor — 10. Naval officer — 11. PZL P-11 — 12. P-23 Karas — 13. Breast insignia for air force

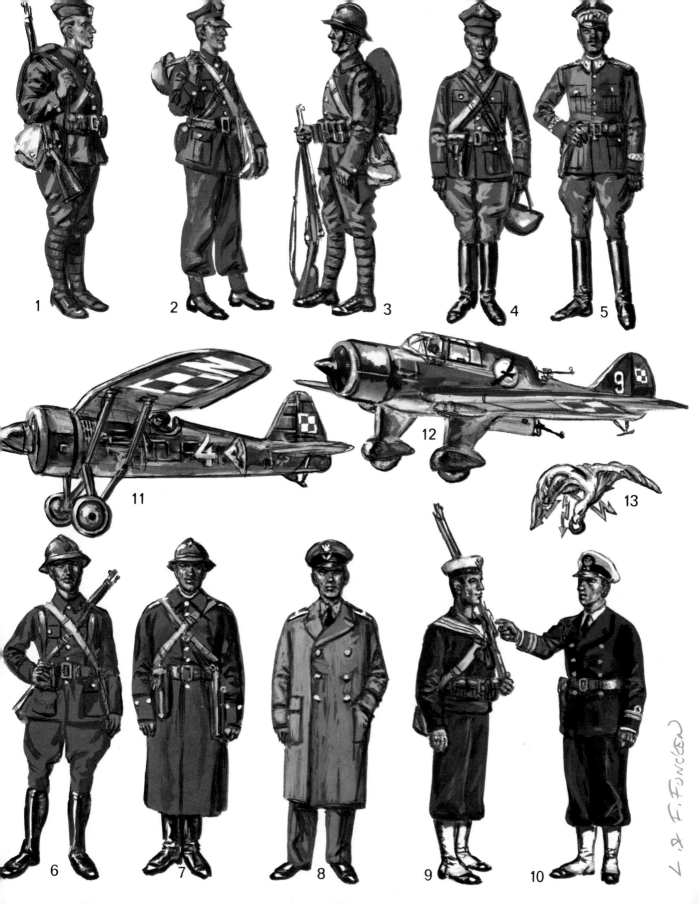

1

2

3

4

5

11

12

13

6

7

8

9

10

L. & F. FUNCKEN

In spite of this speech Hitler still thought that British and French intervention was most improbable and resolved on action. But one final touch to Hitler's plans had to be made: his ensurance of complete freedom of action in the east by negotiating the neutrality of the Soviet Union. This same idea had in fact already occurred to France and Britain but from a different viewpoint. Together with the other eastern European countries, the Soviet Union would be a partner capable of ensuring a mutually cooperative front against eventual attack by Hitler's troops. But neither Poland nor Rumania, any more than Finland or the Baltic countries, would agree to allow Red troops of any kind into their territories. Besides, the successive capitulations of the capitalist countries to Hitler's demands had convinced the Russians that they were trying to divert the Führer's appetite for 'essential space' towards the east. Thus it was that on 23 August 1939 the German-Soviet non-aggression pact was sealed; an 'unnatural alliance' which to some still seems inexplicable. As agreed in a secret clause of this pact, in reward for her non-involvement the Soviet Union was to receive half of the territory of the next victim.

intervention of Britain and France in the west, when Germany would be forced to do battle on two fronts simultaneously.

Field Marshal Śmigly-Rydz accordingly drew up his army along the Polish-German border. Apart from the operational Narew group, stationed far off to the east along the eastern Prussian frontier, their ranks included six armies, each one designated by a geographical name. The Modlin army stationed to the west of the Narew group guarded the frontier south of eastern Prussia. The Pomorze (Pomeranian) army, still further west, controlled the Polish and Danzig territory between eastern Prussia and Pomerania. The dangerous western salient was occupied by the Poznań army. Further south the Łódź and Kraków armies covered the borders with Silesia, and finally, in the south, the Carpathians army kept watch on the borders with Bohemia, Moravia and Slovakia.

On paper, the Polish could muster thirty infantry divisions, eleven cavalry brigades, one tank

THE BLITZKRIEG

Without any preliminary declaration, the 'lightning war' struck Poland at 0445 hours on 1 September 1939. The famous *Blitzkrieg*, which the master of the Third Reich was using for the first time in history, had begun.

The great Clausewitz[1] himself had demonstrated the hollowness of the theory put forward by certain philanthropists, men who still thought that it was possible to conquer an enemy without paying a terrible price in blood. The world's strategists were of the same mind as Clausewitz, and on 1 September 1939 the Poles above all could see no alternative but to attempt to halt the enemy at the frontier and inflict on him the heaviest possible losses. The land inevitably lost to the enemy would then be gradually regained once the initial attack had been halted, and after the

1 The Prussian military theorist (1780-1831), whose doctrine was based on studies of the campaigns of Frederick II and Napoleon.

POLISH ARMY II

Rank insignia and hats: 1. Marshal — 2. General officer's cap — 3. Lieutenant-general — 4. Major-general — 5. Brigadier-general — 6. Colonel — 7. Lieutenant-colonel — 8. Major — 9. Captain — 10. Lieutenant — 11. Second lieutenant — 12. Junior probationary officer — 13. Company sergeant-major — 14. Sergeant — 15. Platoon chief — 16. Corporal — 17. Private — 18. Lance-corporal — 19. Air force cap insignia — 20. Army cap insignia — 21. Senior officer's cap — 22. Junior officer's cap — 23–24. NCO's cap — 25. Ordinary soldier's cap — 26. Old-style helmet — 27. New-style helmet — 28. Collar patch 19th Lancers — 29. Collar patch 27th Lancers — 30. Forage cap — 31. Collar patch 5th light cavalry — 32. Collar patch armoured vehicles — 33. Bread box — 34. Pack

Naval ranks: 35. Admiral — 36. Vice-admiral — 37. Rear-admiral — 38. Commodore — 39. Frigate captain — 40. Corvette captain — 41. Ship's lieutenant — 42. 1st-class ensign — 43. 2nd-class ensign — 44. Junior probationary officer — 45. Chief petty officer — 46. Petty officer — 47. 2nd-class petty officer — 48. Leading seaman — 49. Seaman

brigade—but all out-dated models, badly armoured and slow,[1] and without a single heavy AFV—plus several heavy artillery and engineer units. The air force .possessed only about six hundred aircraft, again mainly of an out-of-date design. The enemy had a crushing superiority, both in quality of machinery and in numbers: forty tank divisions, four motorised divisions, one cavalry brigade and a modern air force of about fifteen hundred machines.[2]

Attacked on all sides by a highly organised infantry reinforced by armoured vehicles, and cut off from the rear by shattering bomb attacks, the Poles defended themselves with ferocious energy. They even managed to hold their own against the enemy, where at Westerplatte[3] for example the arsenal and its 270-strong defence held out for five days against land, sea and air attacks. Nevertheless, by the end of a week of furious battle the Poles found themselves almost entirely surrounded in a large pocket from which their attempts to escape were in vain. There are many tales of Polish cavalry charges against German tanks, but it must be pointed out that these charges were quite obviously directed against the accompanying infantry and not the tanks and armoured cars themselves, a fact which in no way belittles the courage of these valiant cavalrymen.

Pressed into opening a second front as quickly as possible, the Franco-British allies, who had declared war on Germany on 3 September, did not launch the massive offensive that the Poles were so fervently hoping for, though France carried out several cautious operations in the Saar, and the British bombarded the Germans from the air, but this time with nothing more explosive than six million leaflets, the object of which was to convince them of the danger into which their leader was dragging them. True enough, but not of much help to the Poles.

On 17 September Stalin sent his troops into Poland and the end was in sight. Warsaw held out until 27 September, the small Polish fleet surrendered on 1 October, and the last soldiers laid down their arms on 6 October. The sharing out of the spoils had already

But the stubborn pessimists did not have to wait long for their doubts to be vindicated. In 1933 Germany claimed the right to triple the number of her army of a hundred thousand men, the maximum number as laid down by the Treaty of Versailles, and when the League of Nations refused to authorise this Germany stormed out of the conference chamber. taken place on 28 September. The Reich ceded itself 180,000 square kms of the land, well endowed with mines and factories and supporting some twenty-two million inhabitants. The operation had cost them fifteen thousand men, 217 tanks, and about 569 aircraft.[4] The *Blitzkrieg* had been decidedly profitable.

Belgium and the 'Yellow Plan'[5]

Since the end of the First World War the Belgian army had done nothing but submit itself to restrictions and cuts, all of them deemed reasonable in the context of the euphoric pacifism which was sweeping over Europe. The eleven fighting divisions of 1917 had been cut to eight by 1924, and to six by 1926. After all, did not the Treaty of Locarno, which had just been signed the year before, justify such measures? People believed that the relaxed atmosphere among Europe's erstwhile enemies created by this treaty would eliminate the possibility of war for many years. Only the most confirmed pessimists could doubt this.

Germany, France, Belgium, Great Britain and Italy thus solemnly engaged to make peace reign in western Europe and to honour the latest agreements, particularly those relating to Germany and her Polish and Czechoslovakian neighbours. Confidence and goodwill were such that the occupied Rhineland territories were evacuated five years before the required date.

---

1 Built from the Vickers Carden-Loyd chassis to a Belgian design.
2 These figures vary considerably according to source.
3 A small flat peninsula making up part of the town of Danzig.

4 The total Polish losses, civilian and military, have never finally been established.
5 See p. 50.

Then in 1936 Germany reoccupied the Rhineland herself, thus deliberately violating the treaty.

Before the rebirth of German militarism in the early 1930s, Belgium had already been making certain discreet modifications to her defence system and had modernised and strengthened the Meuse Line fortresses. At the same time the Ardennes Light Infantry Corps had been created to ensure better defences on the eastern frontier. The army's weapons had been improved by the modification of the 1889 model rifle, the adoption of a new machine gun, and the establishment of motorised cavalry bases. Then Germany's flagrant violation of the Treaty of Locarno, and the absence of any reaction from the principal signatories, decided the Belgian government to break away from its complacent partners and to pursue a completely independent military policy. The Belgians no longer intended to be drawn automatically into any future armed conflict, and on 14 October 1936 King Leopold III clearly stated his resolve to set up a force within his kingdom capable of dissuading his powerful neighbours from using Belgian territory as a common battle ground. France, Great Britain and even Germany (so she claimed at least) respected the Belgians' decision and professed their intention to honour agreements of assistance to Belgium made at Locarno.

The Belgian government put its new independent policy into practice through a series of military reforms. These reforms included the extension of military service from twelve to seventeen months; the creation of two regiments of motor cyclists for border patrol; the building of three additional forts at Neufchâteau, Battice and Eben-Emael; and the creation of an anti-tank defence line called the KW line—Koningshooikt and Wavre. Armaments continued to improve. New anti-tank guns were introduced and the GTA (Territorial Air Defence) was established, designed to defend forts and large urban centres such as Antwerp, Ghent, Brussels and Liège.[1] With all this, and the mechanisation of a division of *Chasseurs Ardennais* (Ardennes Infantry) and two cavalry divisions, the Belgian army had soon achieved impressive results for such a small state.

1 This artillery will be discussed in more detail in vol. 2.
2 The origin of this expression dates from the Spanish Civil War. The attack on Madrid was undertaken by four pro-Franco columns, the fifth being made up of nationalist factions already inside the city.

MOBILISATION

Events in 1938 brought about preliminary mobilisation, but it was short-lived. Then on 25 August 1939 there was another alert, which this time was to be drawn out until the fatal 10 May 1940. The mobilisation was carried out in consecutive groups from A to E, in such a way that only certain classes and categories of reserves were called up and the economic life of the country was not disrupted. Certain serious deficiencies, however, were not long in showing themselves, the chief being a shortage of officers, the lack of experienced reserve officers, and the difficulty—not to say impossibility—of adequately equipping a large body of reserves.

Worn out by fatigue duties, reduced to navvies rather than turned into soldiers by the exhausting physical work they were forced to do, and demoralised by the increasingly insecure life of their families at home because of shortages of food, the soldiers gradually lost their fighting spirit. This general discontent forced the government to grant leave to farm workers and miners, and then to teachers and certain groups of white-collar workers, a measure which further eroded the already troubled coordination between the units. The enemy did not fail to exploit such a situation, which from their point of view was ideal, and they very soon had their 'fifth column'[2] in the field. But their spies were less effective than the subversive activities of a Belgian group, who were undermining the army from within.

THE ATTACK

The last alert before the great onslaught was on 1 May 1940 at 2100 hours. Important troop and vehicle movements had been reported along the German frontier and a full general alert was given three hours later. The Belgian army consisted of:

6 active infantry divisions

6 first-reserve infantry divisions

6 second-reserve infantry divisions

2 divisions of *chasseurs ardennais,* one of which was motorised

2 cavalry divisions (motorised and cycles)

5 artillery regiments

1 brigade of frontier cyclists

1 brigade of cyclists

1 brigade of mounted cavalry

2 light regiments of *gendarmerie*

3 air force regiments

2 regiments of anti-aircraft troops

plus various other formations of troops and services for the army and army corps. In total, these combined forces amounted to about 650,000 men.

On 10 May the airports, railway stations and communication networks were attacked by tight waves of bombers of the IVth *Fliegerkorps,* without any declaration of war or even ultimatum. Taken by surprise—it was 0400 hours—the Belgian air force, still grounded, lost half its machines in a few minutes.

On land, the Germans crossed the frontier between Malmedy and Burg Reuland and attacked the *chasseurs ardennais,* while gliders dropped four hundred parachute troops, the latest thing in modern warfare, behind the Belgian line. The *chasseurs ardennais* suddenly found themselves attacked from both the front and rear, but despite this the valiant green berets maintained their composure. Wiping out the parachute troops, they also managed to hold off the invading troops, even halting an armoured column for almost five hours. At the same time, however, more German parachutists brought off a magnificent coup on the bridges over the Albert Canal and at the Eben-Emael fortress. The Belgians had seen the strange 'silent aircraft' slipping through the night sky, and when they saw the parachutists jump they eagerly fired upon them, only to discover that they were

dummies. Meanwhile the gliders had continued on their way and landed silently near their real targets—in the case of Eben-Emael actually on the superstructure of the fortress— immediately entering into the attack. Two or three bridges fell undamaged into enemy hands in spite of counter-attacks in which the 2nd regiment of grenadiers was annihilated. The fortress of Eben-Emael held out with difficulty until the next day, 11 May.

THE IMPREGNABLE FORTRESS

The staggering success of the German paratroopers at Eben-Emael was due not only to their courage and the benefits of surprise which they reaped during the assault: five months previous to the attack, pioneer parachutists from the Koch assault section had begun intensive training in preparation for the day. For the attack was to be launched against a showpiece, which the Belgians had been working on for several years.

BELGIAN ARMY 1939-1940 I

1. Automatic rifle FN system Browning model 1930, 7·65 mm — 2. FN motor cycle: the automatic rifle could be attached to the sidecar — 3. Motorised cavalry officer wearing the first pattern leather jacket — 4. General officer — 5. CSLR (candidat-sous-lieutenant de réserve) adjudant. The right to wear the officer's tunic and carry a sabre went with this rank — 6. FN carbine 1924 — 7. 1924 rifle — 8. 1935 rifle. All three were FN 7·65 mm calibre — 9. Browning FN 9 mm with special butt

10. Motorised personnel, Ardennes light infantry — 11. Ardennes light infantryman — 12. Frontier motor cyclist — 13. Light machine-gun carrier — 14. DBT grenade thrower — 15. Schmeisser-Bayard model 34 sub-machine gun, manufactured in Belgium by the Anciens Établissements Pieper at Herstal. Schmeisser had been unable to develop his invention in Germany because of the restrictions imposed by the occupation forces, so he had sold one of his first *Maschinenpistole* to Belgium. After May 1940 this excellent weapon was included in the Wehrmacht arsenal.

1

2

3   4   5

6   7

8

9

10   11

12

13

14

15

L·P
BNCKEN

They were determined to make this a stronghold which would resist even the most violent assault. The tragic experiences of the Liège and Namur fortresses in 1914 had not been forgotten, and this time even the heaviest German howitzers and the most powerful rockets would be unable to blast a way through to casemates buried forty metres below the earth.

This enormous fortress measured eight hundred by nine hundred metres. Its towers, double armoured with 120 and 75 guns, and its triple casemates could pinpoint and wipe out all comers from the Albert Canal to Maestricht. Nor would the enemy have any better chance at night, as the fortress was equipped with extremely powerful spotlights, ready to catch them in their blinding beams. Indeed, the fortress was powerful enough to discourage many of Europe's strategists, including those at German HQ. A few of these officers, however, persisted in their view that it was pregnable, and finally they obtained the green light. Among these German stalwarts was the chief of the 7th air division, General Kurt Student, who had been appointed chief of the parachute brigades in 1938.

From November 1939 the troops assigned to putting the Belgian fortress out of action dedicated themselves to an intensive training period. The greatest secrecy was observed, even the soldiers themselves being completely unaware of their final objective, knowing only that it was enormous and full of hidden problems. They called it the 'mountain'. As part of their training, the parachute troops attacked the abandoned positions on the fortified Czech line, and learned to handle powerful explosives, notably the revolutionary 'hollow charge'.[1] Later in their training, a scale model of the fortress was constructed, a careful study of which soon familiarised the troops with their objective; and the extremely tricky problem of transport to it was studied, solved, and then repeatedly practised. Gliders were to be used, which would be towed behind a transport plane by cable, each glider carrying ten men. The gliders were derisorily named 'Leucoplast bombers'[2] because of

the fragility their bodywork. These, then, were the troops which attacked the bridges on the Albert Canal and the Eben-Emael fortress.

Indeed, the fortress was the one point at which no one expected an attack to be launched. It was a daring scheme, and it paid off; soon the colossus was being systematically destroyed—the 75 and 120 guns in casemates or under the towers, the concrete structures for the Belgian infantry, and then the exterior fortifications, which were demolished during the course of the attack. The white flag was raised on 11 May at 1230 hours, the garrison of twelve hundred men having lost sixty-nine lives together with about forty wounded. Total German losses—in exchange for two or three bridges and a formidable fortress—were thirty-eight dead and one hundred wounded out of a total of 413 men. The air force too had played an important role in this success; it was an early example of what daring and perfect coordination between air and ground forces could achieve.

The fall of such a fortress in so short a time suggested to many minds the use of a 'secret weapon'. It was a rumour which the Germans were careful not to dispel.

THE INVASION

Meanwhile the main body of the German invasion force had not been standing idly by, and the first armoured vehicles crossed the Albert Canal on the same day at 1700 hours. The Belgian army had by now re-grouped, but its first counter-attack was

---

1 Using the principle of a parabolic mirror, the force of the explosive was focused on one point, literally pulverising the thickest armour plating. A detailed explanation will be given in vol. 4.
2 A type of adhesive dressing.

immediately smashed by German aircraft. At the same time, the breach in the 'direct cover' continued to widen, the first defensive wall had yielded, and the light regiments (*gendarmerie*) which were hurriedly sent in as reinforcements could not plug the gap, being forced to retreat to a position on the left bank of the Meuse. Then on 12 May the Belgian army extended its retreat to all its other fronts. Nevertheless numerous units, in spite of fierce resistance, surrounded as they were by armoured troops, simply disappeared, and others met a similar fate from the terrible Stuka attacks.[1]

On 14 May the Belgian army once more pulled itself together and, metaphorically linking arms behind the cover of the KW line with its anti-tank defences and concrete fortifications, prepared to defend its country's heart. But on 15 May the sudden collapse of Holland let loose another complete army, the 18th, against the Belgians. Nevertheless they held on valiantly, inflicting heavy losses on the enemy, although the Germans, sadly, had already succeeded in tearing a complete highway through the British Expeditionary Forces, which along with the French had rushed to the aid of Belgium at the opening of hostilities. This breach was to be closed again, but the less fortunate French in the south were forced to withdraw to the Schelde.

Behind the lines indescribable confusion had taken hold. Refugees blocked the roads and slowed up convoys, and obsessional fears of parachute troops and fifth columnists became ever more widespread. Rumour had it, for instance, that the metal hoardings erected by a certain manufacturer of chicory were concealing instructions, planted by German spies, for the armoured columns behind them. In a state of hysteria the people tore them from the walls. Innocent citizens were arrested, particularly the clergy, whom the people suddenly imagined to be Hitlerian agents in disguise. The situation would have been farcical if it had not been so tragic. Several harmless peasants were run through, victims of spy mania, because their naïve curiosity had led them too close to a battery of artillery or their hunger to a mobile kitchen. One uniformed major-general of the Belgian army escaped by a hair's

breadth summary execution, not by the British or French but by the Belgians themselves, who suddenly suspected his identity card of being too small.

On 16 May the withdrawal continued, in good order and still fighting, but the threat now loomed of being surrounded by the Germans; their aim being to catch the Allies in a gigantic steel trap. Then in the next four days the German advance suddenly accelerated, particularly towards the south-west where they reached Abbeville by the evening of 20 May. French HQ now ordered an offensive which was to come from the partly surrounded troops and move towards the south, while the French undertook a similar offensive northwards. But in spite of repeated efforts from the armies in both the north and south, the breach created between them continued to widen; the German breakthrough on the French front at Sedan and on the Meuse was to worsen the situation and be the final cause of the German victory.

BELGIAN ARMY 1939-1940 III

Insignia of rank: 1. Adjudant de 1re classe — 2. Adjudant — 3. 1er sergent-major — 4. Sergent-major — 5. 1er sergent — 6. Sergent — 7. Caporal — 8. Soldat de 1re classe.

Field caps and collar patches (the braiding on the field cap was reminiscent of the pointed hat, the *hussarde*, worn in the First Empire. The long sun-curtain was normally attached to the back and the tassel hung down the front): 9. Line infantry — 10. Grenadiers — 11. Guides — 12. Light infantry, motor-cycle carbineers — 13. Lancers — 14. Light cavalry — 15. Artillerymen — 16. Engineers
NB: When the insignia did not appear on the collar it was worn on the left side of the field cap and on the shoulder straps.

Sleeve insignia: 17. Long-service chevrons (1 chevron represented 4 years of service. It was silver for NCOs, and was not worn by officers) — 18. Qualified signaller in the Engineers. Also worn by telephone engineers, radio operators, and carrier-pigeon handlers in the Engineers — 19. Machine-gun warrant officer. For ordinary soldiers the insignia were copper plated.

20. Ordinary soldier, Engineers — 21. Engineers Sergeant-major

Regimental insignia: 22. Light regiments — 23. VIIth artillery corps — 24. Spotting section, artillery — 25. Artillery park — 26. Military railway maintenance — 27. Anti-aircraft artillery — 28. Regiment of the Signals — 29. Line infantry and fortress regiments — 30. Transport corps — 31. Flying school — 32. Air force ground crew — 33. Camouflage section

1 This is discussed further in vol. 2.

2

3

4

5 6 7 8

9

10

11

12

13

14

15

16

17 18 19

20 21

22

23

24

25

26

27

28

29

30

31

32

33

L×FFoncken

By 22 May, after over a week of continuous fighting, the Belgian troops were reaching the point of total exhaustion. They were certainly in no condition to take part in an Allied counter-attack in the south, an offensive which in any case, if they were to be in a position to back up the British and French troops, would have meant that they would have had to extend their line to a ruinous ninety kilometres. On 23 May, however, the decision was made to abandon the counter-attack; the British loss of Cambrai, followed by their abandonment of Arras, clearly foretold the Dunkirk evacuation. The Belgians themselves closed ranks on the Lys, keeping Ostend and Nieuport as their only bases.

The Germans were anxious to reach Dunkirk and attacked relentlessly. The battle of the Lys, the first and only great defensive battle of the Belgian war, had begun. It was an action in which the Belgian army was to sacrifice itself, but at the beginning a mere twelve divisions were able to hold off a furious onslaught from twenty enemy divisions, now full of confidence inspired by their past successes and with the additional advantage of being complete masters of the air.

From 24 to 27 May the battle was fierce. The stubborn resistance of the Belgians infuriated the Germans, who wanted to capture the main body of the French and British armies, and they now launched a formidably concentrated air attack. Still the Belgians would not budge. King Leopold's appeal to his forces—'Belgium expects you to do honour to her flag'—had not been in vain. On 26 May the enemy brought up fresh troops, corps after corps being increased, but a request for a counter-offensive from the British got no support—in fact the British Expeditionary Forces had already begun their evacuation. The German planes skimmed over the Belgian defences, wreaking havoc, and on 27 May King Leopold drew upon his last three reserve regiments. But the Germans were too strong. The gaps in the line grew bigger under the growing pressure from an enemy whose will to win seemed to harden the greater their losses became. Munitions were becoming scarce; the end was approaching. One group, completely surrounded, fought itself free with bayonets. The 150 mm artillery was completely wiped out. Behind the lines the disorder was appalling.

Thousands of wounded were being abandoned in railway stations and in some hospitals deserted by the nursing staff.

That same 27 May, at 1530 hours, the King informed the leaders of the Allied mission of his intention to ask for a ceasefire. At 2200 hours the enemy issued its reply: a demand for an immediate 'unconditional surrender'. But the last gun shot was not fired until 28 May at 0600 hours: in the east of the country, completely cut off from the rest of the army, the fortress at Pepinster still held out.

One astonishing fact was that of all the flags and standards belonging to the Belgian army, not one fell into the hands of the enemy. One, that of the 1st light cavalry, was taken to England and became the emblem of the Belgian Armoured Cars Squadron which, four years later, was to take part in the Normandy landings.

BELGIAN ARMY 1939-1940 IV

Caps: 1. General officers — 2. Senior officers up to the rank of major, inclusive — 3. Junior officers and NCOs; regimental insignia were gold for officers and silver for NCOs

Ranks, tunic insignia: a) general officers: 4. Lieutenant général; 5. Général-major — b) senior officers: 6. Colonel; 7. Lieutenant-colonel; 8. Major — c) junior officers: 9. Capitaine-commandant; 10. Capitaine; 11. Lieutenant; 12. Sous-lieutenant

Rank and specialist insignia on the cape or overcoat: 13. Colonel breveté d'état-major serving with HQ (Colonel holding a Staff College certificate) — 14. Major of 14th line regiment — 15. Capitaine-commandant of the 2nd light regiment — 16. Capitaine en premier (senior captain), medical officer of the 1st light cavalry regiment — 17. Capitaine du CT, army artillery — 18. Capitaine, medical officer, 2nd grenadiers regiment — 19. Capitaine, frontier motor-cyclists regiment — 20. Lieutenant, line regiment posted to a Mi. C. Avi. unit of the Transport Corps, 3rd Infantry — 21. Lieutenant, 1st Guides regiment — 22. Lieutenant, administration officer of the Transport Corps of 2nd Infantry — 23. Lieutenant, medical officer of the 12th battalion of engineers — 24. Lieutenant, 3rd Ardennes light infantry regiment — 25. Lieutenant, with Staff College certificate, posted to the fortress regiment at Namur — 26. Artillery lieutenant posted to the directorate of engineers and fortifications — 27. Sous-lieutenant, 3rd light infantry regiment — 28. Sous-lieutenant, Transport Corps of 2nd Infantry — 29. Adjudant de 1re classe, secretary-archivist posted to Quartermaster General of 4th Army Corps — 30. Adjudant posted to the 4th auxiliary troops regiment — 31. Junior ranks, 5th line regiment — 32. Junior ranks, Transport Corps of 3rd Infantry

PART TWO

ARMOURED VEHICLES

French Armoured Vehicles

Since the final ceasefire on 11 November 1918, the incentive for the victors to develop new armoured weapons had gradually diminished. In France, however, the indefatigable General Estienne, creator of the assault ordnance and tanks of the First World War, had come round to the idea of a new type of tank, the B1.

A design for this new tank was settled upon in 1926 and the construction of a prototype was completed in 1929, several models of the B1 being tested in 1931. The objections to it were numerous, for each branch of the fighting forces wanted to use the tank according to its own particular tactics. For the infantry, the tank had to be a support, advancing at the same pace as the assault waves; for the cavalry—always very attached to its horses—the tank had to play only an auxiliary part in their traditional missions of reconnaissance and the protection of the infantry. The artillery branches also had their own requirements, and looked askance at a gun given to any other branch but their own. The B1 was accordingly modified into a 'tank of all work' called the B2, which had to be usable at all stages of combat; an intermediary type, the B1 *bis*, covered the intervening period. It immediately became apparent, however, that the B1 *bis* and B2, although excellent in many ways, were not only extremely costly and difficult to manufacture but were also somewhat slow in comparison with the tanks across the Rhine, whose performances were now beginning to be known.

A series of much lighter vehicles (6 to 20 tons) was also developed and put into service. The cavalry, which had been the last force to accept this type of

'mount', now paradoxically became the best equipped force in this area. Its armoured cavalry divisions were created in 1933 and were subsequently re-named light mechanical divisions. But the fierce individuality of the different forces persisted. Vehicles used for reconnaissance and combat by the cavalry were christened light armoured cars while similar—often identical—vehicles became tanks in the infantry and motorised cannons in the artillery!

MOTORISATION AND MECHANISATION

In the many books devoted to the subject, the reader interested in the events of this period will often come across the expressions 'mechanical division' and 'motorised division'. Though the difference is not easy to define, it is nevertheless an important one: the

DIVISION FROM THE FIRST LINE 1939-1940 (pages 106-107)

1. Reconnaissance groups — 2. Heavy machine guns or anti-tank guns — 3. Front line concrete fortifications — 4. Anti-aircraft artillery — 5. HQ, infantry colonel — 6. First-aid post — 7–10. Cannons of the 75th regiment — 11. HQ, général, divisional infantry — 12. First-aid post — 13. Group of cannon from the 155th regiment — 14. Artillery park — 15. Divisional field HQ — 16. Radio-telegraphy company — 17. Divisional first-aid post — 18. 155th artillery HQ — 19. Cannons of the 155th — 20. Regimental colonel, 75th regiment — 21. Divisional artillery GHQ — 22. Army anti-aircraft defence — 23. Anti-aircraft artillery — 24. Company of the motor baggage train

FRENCH ARMOURED VEHICLES 1939-1940 I

1. Renault FT 17 — 2. D1 — 3. D2 — 4. R35 — 5. FCM — 6. Infantryman, AFVs — 7. Infantryman in walking-out dress, AFVs — 8. Helmet badge, tank teams — 9. Collar patch, infantryman, AFVs — 10. Beret insignia — 11. Collar patch, tank engineer

1

2

3

4

5

6

7

10

503

6

11

L. xf. Funcken

mechanical division was made up of transport troops utilising motorised AFVs in tactics specially designed for their use; the motorised divisions used the AFVs, on wheels or on tracks, to transport troops who then engaged in combat without their usual tactics being modified by the presence of the vehicles. In short, motorisation related to transport, not to fighting.

TANK TACTICS

According to French High Command the close-support infantry tank, armoured against infantry bullets and shell bursts, should (as its name suggests) advance with the foot soldiers and open up for them a path through the first enemy lines. These close-support tanks worked in groups of five, made up of three tanks with guns and two machine-gun tanks. One company numbered twenty tanks, a battalion seventy to eighty tanks.[1]

Breakthrough tanks, protected by their powerful armour plating, had to go into combat before light tanks to make the first thrust through the anti-tank missiles. The heaviest type of tank was reserved for special missions requiring particularly powerful armaments.

To supply the infantry with the ammunition on which they were so dependent the special *chenillette* (carrier) was devised. This consisted of a 400 to 500 kilogram tractor and a 500 to 600 kilogram towing vehicle capable of transporting the equivalent of up to fifty porters' loads of ammunition along the line of fire. These *chenillettes* were easy to handle and were able to scale slopes of up to 1 in 2 as well as being able to cope with quite deep ditches. Ten of these *chenillettes* were allocated to each active battalion.

The cavalry, whose primary quality had to be mobility, was followed by its mechanical units, which had to intervene when the mounted soldiers at the front encountered too fierce opposition.

An army corps or divisional reconnaissance group could muster horse squadrons each equipped with eighteen guns, sections of machine gunners with four

guns, two mortars, and a 37 mm anti-tank gun; and a motorised squadron consisting of a hundred to a hundred and fifty motor cycles, four light armoured cars and a TSF car. One cavalry division was made up of four horse regiments and six horse batteries, three battalions of dragoons and three batteries of towing vehicles, one company of motor-cycle sappers, and three squadrons of light armoured cars making thirty-six vehicles in all.

On page 112 is given a detailed list of France's AFVs in 1940. To this list should be added the old and out-dated Renault FT 17s, small tanks from the First World War. More than fifteen hundred of these were still operational in 1940, and those seized by the Germans were to continue their career in North Africa until 1942.

PAINTWORK AND MARKINGS ON TANKS

During the short 1939-40 campaign considerable imagination was shown in the creation of the distinguishing marks which were painted on tanks. Their basic paintwork too showed distinct differences.

FRENCH ARMOURED VEHICLES 1939-1940 II

1. H 35 bearing the insignia of the 4th cuirassiers regiment, 1st light mechanical division — 2. Panhard 178 armoured car — 3. Cavalry AFV known as reconnaissance armoured car, model 33, with the insignia of the 3rd regiment of cavalry armoured cars

4. Old-style helmet, still being worn in certain units — 5. Helmet, 1935 model, with mica ear-flaps. The same helmet was worn by anti-aircraft teams, but without the ear-flaps.

6. Section chief's pennon — 7. Sous-officer adjoint (right-hand tank), pennon — 8. Pennon, second tank (left-hand) — 9. Company commandant's pennon (the pennon sometimes had a white horizontal band carrying the company insignia) — 10. Breakdown pennon (both for mechanical failures and enemy damage)

---

1 On the declaration of war the tank combat regiments were divided into autonomous battalions. The 155th regiment of combat tanks at Verdun, for example, became the 9th battalion (R35 tanks) and the 37th battalion (B1 *bis* tanks).

FRENCH ARMOURED VEHICLES, 1940

TYPE	TON-NAGE	ARMAMENT	CREW	SPEED	RANGE	USES
Cavalry AFVs Reconnaissance armoured cars A.M.R. 1933 model	6	1 7·5 machine gun	2	55 km/h	200 km	382 vehicles in 1940—light mechanical divisions of automitrailleuses
A.M.R. 1935 model	6	a 25 cannon or m. gun (13·2) and 1 m. gun (7·5)	2	55 km/h	200 km	automitrailleuses of certain infantry division reconnaissance groups
Armoured combat car A.M.C. Somua or Somua tank	20	1 cannon (47) 1 m. gun (7·5)	3	45 km/h	200 km	261 vehicles in 1940, mainly in squadrons of light mechanical division regiments
Light Tanks D1 tank	13	1 cannon (47) 1 m. gun (7·5)	3	45 km/h		150 models—North Africa
D 2 tank	18.5	as above	3	45 km/h		90 models—1 battalion of general reserves, 3 N. African battalions
Renault Tanks R 35	9.8	1 cannon (37) 1 m. gun (7·5)	2	20 km/h	140 km	about 1,000 models in 1940—fighting tank battalions
R 39	10.4	1 cannon (37) 1 m. gun (7·5)	2	20 km/h	140 km	
Hotchkiss tanks H 35	11.4	1 cannon (37) 1 m. gun (7·5)	2	42 km/h	130 km	800 vehicles in all in 1940—reserve cuirassier divisions, squadrons of light mechanical divisions, tank battalions accompanying infantry
H 39	12	1 cannon (37) 1 m. gun (7·5)	2	42 km/h	150 km	
FCM 36 tank (Forges et Chantiers de la Méditerranée)	12	1 cannon (37)	2	23 km/h	320 km	100 models were built—fighting tank battalions
Heavy tanks Break-through tanks 2C	68	1 cannon (75) 4 m. guns (7·5)	12	13 km/h	100 km	6 destroyed without fighting by Stuka
Manœuvres tank B1	31	1 cannon (75) 1 cannon (37) 2 m. guns (7·5)	4	28 km/h	200 km	modified in 1931 to make the B1 *bis*
B1 *bis*	32	1 cannon (75) 1 cannon (47)	4	29 km/h	140 km	270—tank battalions of the reserve cuirassier divisions
B2	32	1 cannon (75) 1 cannon (47) 2 m. guns (7·5)	4	28 km/h	140 km	these equipped 3 battalions of fighting tanks

FRENCH ARMOURED VEHICLES 1939-1940 III

1. Somua or S35 fighting armoured car. This was the best of all the French AFVs of the time — 2. B1 *bis* — 3. Break-through tank 2 C — 4. Renault infantry bren-gun carrier

5. Armoured vehicles officer in full dress — 6. Officer in battle dress

1

2

3

4

5

6

L. & F.
FUNCKEN

Paintwork

In early 1940 the order was given to paint all AFVs a matt army grey or green—up to this date all vehicles had been camouflaged by the application of large irregular shaped patches of the three colours brown, grey-green and ochre—but there was no time for this measure to be fully carried out. After the disaster in Belgium and the breakthrough at Sedan a third type of camouflage appeared on the field—those vehicles which had been sent as reinforcements direct from the factories, hastily painted only in various shades of grey.

Markings

Close-support tanks carried a white painted grenade on the chassis marked with the figures 1, 2 or 3, in red or black, which indicated the weight category of the vehicle for transport by rail. The B tanks usually had a name inscribed on the turret or body (sometimes on both) such as *Bayard, Rhône, Cher, Languedoc, Dunkerque,* etc. These names were also worn by certain units of the Army Service Corps on a tab fastened above the upper left pocket of the uniform.

As a result of the first engagements with the enemy, it was realised that there was a need to distinguish the tanks of the different troops and accordingly these were marked with large capital letters or with two-figure numbers starting with 01. The national tricolour cockade did not appear in any regular position. Usually it was to be found on the turret or the cupola (the semi-spherical appendage on top of the tank turret), but on the cavalry tanks could also appear on the front or on the back. The battalion insignia, or that of the regiment, might also be displayed, according to the whims of the individual unit chiefs. For example, in the 9th tank battalion a skull and crossbones decorated the front right mudguard. The ace of hearts, spades, diamonds or clubs, painted directly on to the ground colour in either solid red or blue or outlined with a fine white line, were also often seen. In fact the only systematic use of such markings was to be found on the small FT 17s, where each company was distinguished by a geometric figure painted in white. These were:

1st company: circle, 35 cm diameter

2nd company: square of 30 cm
3rd company: triangle, isosceles with 45 cm base
4th company: lozenge with diagonal of 45 cm

In each company thus distinguished the four sections were differentiated in the following way:

1st section: ace of spades, painted in blue
2nd section: ace of hearts, painted in red
3rd section: ace of diamonds, painted in red
4th section: ace of clubs, painted in blue

These marks still appear on certain modern tanks, though in a less conspicuous form, reflecting their commanders' continuing attachment to the old armoured vehicles.

German Armoured Vehicles, 1939-41

In 1918 Germany was far behind her opponents in the design and manufacture of armoured vehicles, but by 1939 was easily the most advanced in this same area. The principal agent of this extraordinary reversal was an officer of the Reichswehr, General Heinz Guderian. In the face of accepted dogma about the castellated tank and infantry close-support tank, this imaginative officer applied himself to creating a unique—perhaps revolutionary is a better word—armoured division, the *Panzerdivision*, which was made up of various types of tank capable of short-, medium-, or long-range fighting, in close liaison with motor-cycle

GERMAN ARMOURED CARS 1939-1941

1. Kfz model 13 — 2. Model 222 — 3. Model 231 — 4. Model 231 with eight wheels

1

2

3

4

L.&F.Funcken

gunners, mounted gunners, and an equally mobile anti-tank artillery.

General Guderian never attempted to conceal the fact that he had developed much of his theory from a close study of the *Provisional Instruction on Tanks and Armoured Cars* which had been in use in the British army since 1927. Like all enlightened innovators, the general's task was made even more difficult by the dogged resistance to his ideas of enemies and sceptics. In 1933, however, he won the enthusiastic support of the Führer, who was able to appreciate all the advantages of this new fighting force.

THE ARMOURED DIVISION

General Guderian, then, had finally been given a free hand and was now able to start putting his ideas into practice. In 1935 he got under way his first three German *Panzerdivisionen,* each one made up of:

1 Motorised reconnaissance group

a One attached company made up of one section of light armoured cars and one section of liaison motor cyclists.

b Two companies of light and heavy armoured cars: forty vehicles in all.

c One company of motor cyclists with nine machine guns and four heavy machine guns.

d One support company with two 76 mm mortars and three 37 mm anti-tank guns.

2 Tank brigade

a One HQ.

b One command section with reconnaissance car and motor cyclists.

c Two tank regiments each of two battalions, subdivided into four companies comprising thirty-two light and medium tanks, plus forty-nine command tanks, making a total of 561 machines.

d One support company with one heavy machine gun, two 75 mm mortars and three 37 mm anti-tank guns.

3 Brigade of fusiliers

Intended as a support for the tanks, and as an occupation force for conquered territory, the fusiliers had one regiment and one battalion of motor cyclists. The regiment, of two battalions, was transported in general purpose lorries. Each battalion was made up of three companies armed with heavy machine guns, a support company with two 75 mm mortars and three 37 mm guns as well as a companion company which had eight heavy armoured cars and ten 80 mm grenade-launchers. The motor-cycle battalion was made up of three companies of fusiliers equipped with nine machine guns and one company with twelve heavy machine guns.

4 Artillery regiment

This regiment carried twelve 105 mm guns.

5 Pioneer battalion

This battalion was made up of three pioneer companies, one group of pontoneers or bridge columns, and a light column.

6 Anti-tank battalion

The three companies in this battalion carried thirty-six 37 mm guns drawn by general duty vehicles or special tractors.

7 Signals battalion

This battalion was made up of one telegraph company and one radio company. This whole impressive roll call was further extended by the addition of extra fusilier units on the creation in 1938-9 of the fourth, fifth and sixth *Panzerdivisionen.*

GERMAN ARMOURED VEHICLES 1939-1941 I

1. 35 (t) Czech — 2. 38 (t) Czech — 3. Panzer I model B — 4. Panzer II model C

1

2

3

4

Armoured divisions of 1939-40

When hostilities broke out the German forces were considerably below those cited above, in tanks mustering about three hundred and twenty machines per armoured division. In 1939 an armoured division numbered twelve tank companies and twelve companies of fusiliers.

Light brigades

In 1937-8 four light brigades, each with one battalion of tanks and three battalions of motorised fusiliers, were created independently of the large armoured divisions. After the Plish campaign they were converted into the sixth, seventh, eighth and ninth *Panzerdivisionen*, each comprising one regiment of tanks, of two or three battalions each.

THE 1940 CAMPAIGN

Throughout the 1940 campaign there were ten German divisions in operation, but instead of the line up of forty battalions envisaged by Guderian in 1935, there were only thirty-five, with the battalions themselves much less complete than Guderian's theory had dictated. However, once the overwhelming success of the *Panzerdivisionen* had demonstrated to the German army the value of such a force, a further increase in their divisions had to be the next logical step. The armoured divisions were therefore doubled before the end of 1940, though the actual number of tanks was reduced, an apparent diminution in striking power which was compensated for by the appearance of two new kinds of more powerful tank.

THE RUSSIAN CAMPAIGN

On the eve of Barbarossa, the *Panzerdivisionen* were made up of no more than six armoured divisions each comprising a single tank regiment of three battalions, plus thirteen divisions of only two battalions. The brigades of fusiliers were made up of two motorised regiments of two battalions plus a motor-cycle battalions each. The accompanying artillery was reinforced by 150 mm howitzers, 150 mm guns, and 88 mm anti-aircraft guns which would eventually make their name as anti-tank guns. The number of tanks had again dropped, now totalling no more than one hundred and fifty to two hundred vehicles, a situation brought about by slow rate of production at home and which was strongly criticised by the commanders-in-chief. So it was that with only seventeen divisions the first attacks were carried out, nevertheless achieving the astonishing successes already described. Two supplementary divisions had been completed and were ready for action, and another was in the process of being formed, but even these twenty divisions could muster no more than forty-six battalions—a long way short of the 1935 forecasts. Future events were to exploit this weakness to the full.

GERMAN ARMOURED VEHICLES 1939-1941 II

1. Panzer III models F, G, and H — 2. Panzer IV model D — 3. NCO, 24th Panzer regiment (distinguishing piping was golden yellow and not to be confused with the lemon yellow of the armoured vehicles signals sections — 4. Armoured vehicles lieutenant in black parade dress (distinctive piping in pink, which was the most usual colour in the armoured divisions)

5. Armoured divisions padded beret — 6. National emblem — 7. Collar patch: the skull-and-crossbones did not imply any connection with the Waffen-SS; it was the badge of the armoured divisions borrowed from the old cavalry regiments — 8. Field cap, other ranks — 9. Officer's field cap (not worn above the rank of colonel)

SUMMARY TABLE OF THE MAIN GERMAN ARMOURED VEHICLES

TYPE[1]	TONNAGE	SPEED	RANGE	ARMS	CREW	CON-STRUCTION DATE
Pz. Kpfw Ia	5.4	37 km/h	145 km	2 7.92 mm machine guns	2	1934
Pz. Kpfw Ib	6	40 km/h	140 km	2 7.92 mm machine guns	2	1935
Pz. Kpfw II a1, a2, b, c	9.5	40 km/h	140 km	1 special 20 mm cannon	3	1935
Pz. Kpfw II d	10	55 km/h	200 km	1 20 mm cannon, 1 7.92 mm machine gun	3	1937
Pz. Kpfw II f	9.5	40 km/h	190 km	1 20 mm cannon, 1 7.92 mm machine gun	3	1941
Pz. Kpfw IIIa	15	32 km/h	150 km	1 37 mm cannon, 3 7.92 mm machine guns	5	1936
Pz. Kpfw IIIb	19.3	40 km/h	165 km	1 37 mm cannon, 3 7.92 mm machine guns	5	1937
Pz. Kpfw IIIe	19.5	40 km/h	175 km	1 50 mm cannon, 2 7.92 mm machine guns	5	1939
Pz. Kpfw IVa	17.3	30 km/h	150 km	1 75 mm cannon, 2 7.92 mm machine guns	5	1936
Pz. Kpfw IVb	17.4	40 km/h	200 km	1 75 mm cannon, 1 7.92 mm machine gun	5	1937
Pz. Kpfw IVd	20	40 km/h	200 km	1 75 mm cannon, 2 7.92 mm machine guns	5	1939
Pz. Kpfw Ive	20	42 km/h	200 km	1 75 mm cannon, 2 7.92 mm machine guns	5	1940
Czechoslovakian tanks 35 t	10.5	40 km/h	190 km	1 37 mm cannon, 2 7.92 mm machine guns	4	1935
38 t	9.5	42 km/h	230 km	1 37 mm cannon, 2 7.92 mm machine guns	4	1938

1 Pz. Kpfw = *Panzerkampfwagen*, HFV

GUNS AND ARMOURY

From the chapters on France and the Soviet Union it has already become clear that castellated tanks of enormous tonnage were of little practical use. Certain experiences of the Spanish Civil War, however, had led to a careful re-examination of the efficiency of relatively small AFVs, and further tests carried out in peacetime had brought experimenters to some pessimistic conclusions as to the resistance of light armoured cars to shell and gun fire, conclusions which were in fact to be completely belied. It was soon realised that there was an enormous difference between concentrated testing under experimental conditions, where the steel plate was hit head-on by the shell which it was meant to resist, and the firing which took place in actual combat, when it happened only on the rarest of occasions that the shell struck it target with maximum impact.[1] The stream-lined tan of free-flowing form, specially developed for use o uneven terrain, almost never appeared on completely horizontal plane with the gun. Thus it ha every chance of deflecting the missile, or at leas damaging it, thereby reducing its effectiveness. Th irrefutable truth of this discovery about ligh armoured vehicles in warfare found furthe confirmation in the tests of strength to which, as th Second World War progressed, they were put throug by the increasingly powerful anti-tank guns.

1 Lieutenant-Colonel Perré, a specialist in French tanks, reckone that the achievement of a direct hit would be little short o miraculous.